Augsburg College
George Sverdrup Library
Minneapolis, Minnesota 55404

VASILY OSIPOVICH KLYUCHEVSKY

An Outline of

MODERN RUSSIAN HISTORIOGRAPHY

By
ANATOLE G. MAZOUR

With an introduction by
ROBERT J. KERNER

UNIVERSITY OF CALIFORNIA PRESS
BERKELEY : 1939

UNIVERSITY OF CALIFORNIA PRESS
BERKELEY, CALIFORNIA

◇

CAMBRIDGE UNIVERSITY PRESS
LONDON, ENGLAND

COPYRIGHT, 1939, BY THE
REGENTS OF THE UNIVERSITY OF CALIFORNIA

PRINTED IN THE UNITED STATES OF AMERICA
BY SAMUEL T. FARQUHAR, UNIVERSITY PRINTER

TITLE IN BCL 2nd ED

TO
L. J. M.
GALLANT, LOYAL COMRADE

CONTENTS

	PAGE
VASILY OSIPOVICH KLYUCHEVSKY	*Frontispiece*
INTRODUCTION, by Robert J. Kerner	vii
PREFACE	ix

THE EIGHTEENTH CENTURY

Introduction	1
Tatishchev	2
Müller	5
Schlözer	8
Shcherbatov	11
Boltin	13
Summary	15

THE NINETEENTH CENTURY AND LATER

Publication of Sources	18
Karamzin	22
Polevoy	29
Pogodin	30
The Westerners and Slavophiles	32
Solovyev	36
Kavelin	41
Klyuchevsky	44
Bestuzhev-Ryumin	51
Platonov	52
Lyubavsky	54
Presnyakov	55
Lappo-Danilevsky	57
Milyukov	59
Semevsky	62

The Nineteenth Century and Later (*Continued*)

	PAGE
Shchapov	68
Kostomarov	71
Hrushevsky	73
Siberian Historiography	75
Shakhmatov	79
Ikonnikov	81
Pavlov-Silvansky	82
Pokrovsky	83
Emigré Historians	98
The Eurasian School	99
Conclusion	105
Notes	108
General Bibliography	123
Index	127

INTRODUCTION

FEW FIELDS of *historiography are more interesting than the Russian and very few are as stimulating. Whether one follows it in the ponderous tomes of Ikonnikov, or in the keen observations of Milyukov, the philosophical analyses of Karyeyev, or the latest Marxist criticisms against Pokrovsky, he is fascinated by the vistas which lead to an understanding of Russia and her historians. In no other national field of historical endeavor is it as vital to see historiography in perspective. Here, without a guide, the student is lost. How Russians wrote history, what philosophical views, foreign and domestic, influenced them, what objectives the schools of Russian historians evolved, and what they accomplished, from Tatishchev to Pokrovsky, from the first national historian to the court historian of the Bolsheviks—all these are essential. What names pass by in review! Karamzin, Kostomarov, Solovyev, Klyuchevsky, Hrushevsky, Platonov, Milyukov, Pokrovsky! From national glorification to national degradation—from the minutest research to wide-sweeping horizons! Perhaps no other nation has a historiography so rich, so varied, so vital, so revealing. It is a legacy of hope and pathos.*

To survey this field with reasonable insight and balance is no mean task. To give it some organization and to sketch its main lines of development requires a broad and discerning use of a wide variety of sources besides the writings of the historians themselves. In devoting himself to this task, Dr. Anatole G. Mazour has rendered not only to Anglo-Saxon students, but to Russians as well, a valuable service.

ROBERT J. KERNER

PREFACE

THIS STUDY *was undertaken at the suggestion of a number of professional colleagues. Upon commencing it, I found at once so great a number of writers to discuss or at least to mention—lest I be accused of ignorance of them—that for a while I wondered if I should not abandon the project, and the difficulty of presenting many of the problems to readers who lack acquaintance with Russian only made me hesitate the more. However, I decided to keep on; and to facilitate the task, I determined to deal with Russian historians of Russian history only, leaving out the contributions which a legion of scholars of that country have made to ancient, Byzantine, and modern history. From the first sentence to the last, I have borne in mind that this work is designed merely as a guide for students who wish to acquaint themselves with Russian historiography. The degree of success attained in this endeavor is to be judged by others than the author.*

I take pleasure in expressing gratitude to Professors Robert J. Kerner of the University of California, George Vernadsky of Yale, and Michael Karpovich of Harvard for their readiness not only to accept the laborious task of reading the manuscript in its raw form, but particularly for sparing neither time nor effort in gathering bibliographical data and correcting errors. I also wish to express my thanks to the University of Chicago Press and the editors of the Journal of Modern History *for allowing me to reprint parts of this outline which appeared as an article in the* Journal *for June, 1937.*

A. G. M.

Berkeley, California, April, 1938.

Modern Russian Historiography

THE EIGHTEENTH CENTURY

Introduction

Russian historiography, though a comparatively new field and representing, as a recent writer has said, a "minor country," is by no means so meager as certain historiographers maintain. It has been and probably still is customary to begin an account of modern Russian historiography with Karamzin (1766–1826)—a totally erroneous notion, which must be dispelled from the outset. A period earlier than that of Karamzin—the eighteenth century—has left a legacy which no student can possibly afford to overlook. The eighteenth century assured to the later historian convenient access to archival material formerly unknown; it was the period of the *Geschichtssammler,* to use the term of Schlözer, which enabled the nineteenth-century *Geschichtserzähler* to exploit more effectively the work of their predecessors. It is chiefly for this reason that any conscientious work on modern Russian historiography must first pay due tribute to the pioneers of the eighteenth century.

The writing of history in Russia began not with the universities or learned societies, but with amateurs. Not until the nineteenth century did history become an organized subject, approached in a systematized fashion and transferred from private study rooms to university seminars, where the teaching and writing of history became the profession of men who devoted themselves exclusively to it. However, those amateurs who had begun to write history in the eighteenth century must not be sneered at. Confronting them was a problem of enormous difficulty—that of discrediting all legendary, unauthenticated material and placing the study on an entirely new and scientific basis, turning back for this purpose to the original documents in order to reconstruct the true story. Formerly, not only had biblical legends been the chief sources for a national interpretation of the elder time; they had also served the purpose of a patriotic justification of the assumed origin of the Slavs as well as of their "glorious past." The earlier writers about Russian beginnings had to liberate themselves from medieval influences, particularly that of the Polish chronicles. The historians of the latter half of the eighteenth century faced a still more difficult task; for they had to dissect a century's accumulation of the distortions of the chroniclers of Moscow and of other local chroniclers of the "appanage" period when all accounts were colored by the prevailing spirit of particularism. It was for a long time that these sources had provided the canvas on which writers embroidered their historical narratives; so one can well comprehend the nature of the struggle in which the modern historian found himself engaged.

Tatishchev (1686–1750).—The father of modern Russian historiography was Vasily N. Tatishchev. He was the first to conceive Russian history on a scale not even imagined by any previous writer; he was the pioneer in endeavoring to construct a pragmatic narrative of the Russian past.[1] A true son

---
[1] Superior figures refer to notes on pp. 108–122.

ject barely touched at that time and one still awaiting due appreciation in Western historical literature.* Müller's publication in German of the *Sammlung russischer Geschichte* further attracted the attention of Western scholars to Russian sources—among them Schlözer; and Müller's *History of Siberia,* though a lifeless account, remains to this day a source to which students refer.†

The opening of the Siberian archives was followed by further investigations in western Russia, especially in the archives of Moscow, which the government was long unwilling to open to curious scholars. In 1748 Müller even consented to abandon his German citizenship (after twenty-three years of residence in Russia!) and become a Russian subject in order to enjoy the possible privilege of access to the archives of the former Moscow Department of Justice, where the majority of fifteenth- and sixteenth-century government records were on file.

In 1766 Catherine II appointed Müller to the superintendency of the Russian archives, a post he had long desired and in which he remained for the rest of his life. During his later years he continued the compilation of all the sources upon which he could possibly lay his hands. His toil was compensated by the fruitful research of later scholars, who began to exploit the material he had so painstakingly prepared. More

---

* In passing it may be noted that Professor Robert J. Kerner, of the University of California, is engaged in writing an extensive history of Russian eastward expansion on the basis of these and other archival materials.

† The reader is referred to an excellent essay entitled "Müller as an Historian," by S. V. Bakhrushin, in the recent edition of Müller's *History of Siberia* (Moscow, 1937), 5–55.

he had not expected. Realizing that his age permitted no ambitious literary undertaking and that archival work demanded unremitting attention, he sought younger men to continue his work, at first among his compatriots—like Schlözer—and later among the rising Russian generation represented by N. N. Bantysh-Kamensky, who succeeded his teacher as Director of the Archives of the former Moscow Department of Foreign Affairs.

Schlözer (1735-1809).—If Müller was the *Geschichtssammler,* August Ludwig von Schlözer was undoubtedly the *Geschichtsforscher.*[15] He was among the first to urge the scientific systematization of all sources upon which critical historical writing might be based. A true scholar, Schlözer saw the necessity of widening the field of history. Müller had already visualized the historian as a man "without a fatherland, without a religion, without a sovereign." Schlözer went farther: he maintained that history must be universal, embracing more than mere political development, and that the historian must abandon his academic isolation for a closer acquaintance with the wide world of reality. Whatever source material the historian finds, Schlözer insisted, must be analyzed objectively; historical writing was to be founded on sources that the historian considered authentic, and the narrative based on these was to be given in an unbiased fashion, regardless of the race or national affiliation of the narrator. "The first law of history," declared Schlözer, "is to state nothing false. It is better not to know than to be deceived."* This new

---
* It is interesting to note that Schlözer emphasized the significance of statistics, which he named "eine stillstehende Geschichte."—*Russky biografichesky slovar,* XXIII, 342.

conception was brought to the very doorstep of the Russian Academy of Sciences by Schlözer at a time when discord between German and non-German members of that institution was at its height, especially between Müller and Lomonosov (1711–1765). It came, also, at a period when growing nationalism was beginning to prejudice Russian historical writing very strongly.

Schlözer had quite incidentally found himself in Russia in 1761, hoping to find some employment which would enable him to proceed with his studies and to travel in the Near East; he also desired to familiarize himself with Russian sources. He was sheltered by Müller, who hoped to exploit him for his own purposes.[16] With the assistance of a man like Schlözer, he thought, he could make use of the documents brought from Siberia and eventually write an extensive history.[17] These documents he guarded jealously from the curious eye of his young assistant. But Schlözer had his own ambitions. In a short time, after many disappointments, he refused to serve longer as an object of exploitation, and broke off relations with his patron. In 1767 he left Russia, presumably on a leave of absence, but after the leave expired (in 1770) he refused to return. He had left Russia with no knowledge of the nature of the documents contained in Müller's assembled materials, and so in his later work on Russian history he continued to follow the outmoded method of relying exclusively on the chronicles rather than the most recent documents. He perceived, however, that a different method of approach must be developed; and his theories in this respect are not without interest.

10   *Modern Russian Historiography*

The history of Russia, according to Schlözer, falls into four periods: (1) R. nascens, 862–1015; (2) divisa, 1015–1216; (3) oppressa, 1216–1462; (4) victrix, 1462–1762. Furthermore, the writing of a complete history of Russia, he believed, was premature unless (1) all national sources (*studium monumentorum domesticorum*) and (2) all sources pertaining to Russia to be found in foreign archives (*studium monumentorum extrariorum*) had first been gathered together and properly edited. He began to work in this direction while at the University of Göttingen. In 1769 he published a list of Russian chronicles entitled *Annallen Russici slavonice et latine cum varietate lectionis ex codd. X Lib. I usque ad annum 879*. This was soon followed by two other works, *Das neue veränderte Russland* and *Allgemeine nordische Geschichte*. In 1802 he undertook the publication of the original text of the *Chronicle of Nestor,* dedicating it to Alexander I.[18] This work inspired Russian scholars with the idea of publishing a complete collection of Russian chronicles—an accomplishment achieved only in the twentieth century.

Schlözer's numerous annotations to the *Chronicle of Nestor* reveal remarkable learning, but also a certain bias for which many Russian historians could never forgive him. For example, he noted that until the Varangians (Germans, of course!) came—and here it was emphasized that they came at the invitation of the Old Slavs, who were unable to establish order—the Slavic tribes were in a state of barbarism. The opinions of Ewers and Storch were quite contrary to this view. Lacking acquaintance with the sources collected by Müller or with the yet undeveloped Russian archeology, Schlözer was naturally bound to make appalling errors. Some of these resulted from his ignorance of the latest achievements in Russia, others from the sheer bitterness of spirit in which he left that country, never to return. He had also suffered unpleasant experiences in his last years in Göttingen, where he was considered an atheist and even a dangerous radical because he had justified the execution of Charles I.[19] Despite many of his errors of interpretation, some of which offended Russian national sentiment, and despite his personally disagreeable traits, such as his boundless self-conceit (with his departure from Russia, according to Schlözer, historical learning came to a standstill!),[20] Russian historiography is indebted to him for a very great enlargement of historical study.[21]

Shcherbatov (1733-1790).—Historical study and the publication of source material became, in the second half of the eighteenth century, the occupation of many members of the Russian élite. The reign of Peter I and the following years of confusion, the struggle against foreign domination in intellectual life, and the endeavor to create in Russia a culture of her own, all conspired to bring this about. On the one hand, there was an ardent effort to write a pragmatic history of Russia; on the other, a desire to explore all archival material in order to justify by documentary evidence every claim to intellectual independence, if not superiority. This was not precisely in agreement with the more universal conception of Schlözer, but, so far at least as students began to search for sources, it coincided with his ideas. Among these students two were preëminent, Prince Mikhail M. Shcherbatov and Major General Ivan N. Boltin.

Prince Shcherbatov was one of the most cultured Russians of his time. He had received an excellent education, was thoroughly familiar with world literature, and had built up an enormous private library. Among his many political and social occupations, Shcherbatov became also intensely interested in Russian history.[22] This was fortunate; for not only was his own library of great assistance, but also access to the state archives, which he enjoyed by special permission of Catherine II, aided him to make greater progress than had his predecessors.[23] Shcherbatov was familiar with many Russian documents of which Schlözer had known nothing, though he had mastered but one foreign language, French. It is to be regretted that the erudition of Schlözer and the aristocratic culture of Shcherbatov could not somehow have been amalgamated; for, in spite of his prodigious industry and excellent opportunities, Shcherbatov sadly lacked skill in handling historical sources, with the result that he made more errors than a careful scholar would have made without any sources at all. His voluminous work had, moreover, a ponderous style which, particularly to a modern reader, is extremely tedious. His *Russian History* is a rehash of the chronicles he had read indiscriminately, and is therefore more of a guide than a study, though Karamzin made good use of it in the early part of the nineteenth century.[24]

Shcherbatov lived during a period when the demarcation between the old and the new Russia was becoming more and more distinct. As a typical aristocrat of the old Russia, in spite of his flirtation with Voltairian philosophy and his being a Freemason, he could see nothing good in the new ideas,

The Eighteenth Century 13

and could only lament the degradation of his fatherland. For him the old Russian customs and institutions held a peculiar virtue which the ruthless onslaught of Western ideas forced by Peter I and the loose morals of Catherine II tended to destroy. His last work, *Concerning the Corruption of Morals in Russia,* is an obituary for the old Russia and an appeal for the preservation of its forgotten virtues. Acknowledging the progress these two sovereigns had assured to Russia, he could not overlook the price which the people had paid for it in the disesteem that had befallen the virtues of the national character in the enthusiasm for Western civilization.

Boltin (1735-1792).—Like Prince Shcherbatov, General Boltin was a representative of the "amateur school." He gave all his spare time, which was none too much, to gathering sources and familiarizing himself with archival material and private collections. This work was greatly assisted by the well-known collector of Russian antiquities, Count A. I. Musin-Pushkin. The "antiquarian dilettantism" of Boltin proved to have a more serious aspect than a superficial observer might have detected. In 1759, Le Clerc, a French physician, visited Russia at the invitation of the court, and on the basis of this visit wrote a history of that country.[25] Le Clerc so deeply hurt Boltin's patriotic pride by numerous misinterpretations that Boltin took up his literary cudgels in defense of his country; and, since Le Clerc had relied greatly on the first two volumes of Shcherbatov's history, Boltin was forced to attack both writers. This criticism resulted in an impressive four-volume work, two volumes for each opponent, in which Boltin displayed not only a profound knowledge of the subject as well as a good deal of erudition, but also an ability for original thought.[26] The criticism of Le Clerc's work impressed Catherine so much that she ordered the two volumes to be published at state expense.

Boltin was one of the earliest historians to attempt to analyze the meaning of historical processes; he held the view, as did Bodin and Montesquieu, that climate is one of the most important factors in determining social and political institutions. Criticizing Le Clerc's thesis that Russia was a barbaric country governed by whimsical despotism, Boltin endeavored to show that, on the contrary, only through their cultural superiority and monarchical form of government did the Russian people succeed in surviving foreign dominance. Like Shcherbatov, he was a typical aristocrat of eighteenth-century Russia, favoring the Muscovite period and was skeptical of the reforms of Peter I and Catherine II,[27] but, unlike Shcherbatov, he demanded that the subject be handled critically. He reminded Shcherbatov in very precise language that if one lacks skill in handling historical sources it is preferable to leave them alone altogether.[28] He also insisted, as had Schlözer, that history can never be rightly written unless all the documents, within the country as well as without, are properly gathered and organized. This was not a task for one person; whoever undertakes to combine the compilation of all sources pertaining to national history with the writing of that history is bound to fail, as had Tatishchev and Müller.

Boltin strongly influenced many of the later nineteenth-century Russian writers. He was particularly admired by the later Slavophile school, which held history to be a science of

Modern Russian Historiography

Commission a mass of material which the Commission continued to publish for the next century and a half. Though begun incidentally, Müller's collection of manuscripts from the Siberian archives, known as "Müller's Portfolios" (258 in all and for the most part still unpublished), opened a mine of sources from which students of Russian history, particularly of Russia's eastward expansion, draw material to this day.[13] The originals of many of those documents can no longer be found, so that Müller's copies remain in large part the only available records of Siberian history.

Until Müller's work appeared, almost all the historians had based their studies chiefly if not solely upon the only chronicles known to them. Müller's material, which makes up the larger part of the later Supplements to *Akty istoricheskiye*,[13] revealed new and more reliable sources, including numerous government decrees, orders, charters, and official correspondence. His papers contained extracts from the chronicles of the early seventeenth century, various statistical data, sources pertaining to Siberian ethnography and geography, and descriptions of the more important expeditions and personal adventures in eastern Siberia.[14] Besides these new documents, he was the first to direct attention to totally unknown Tartar and Mongolian sources; he recorded many oral versions of the obscure past, and collected archeological, linguistic, and genealogical data. His discoveries led to an increasing interest in further search for archival material as well as in historical writing, particularly concerning later periods of Russian history. Moreover, they gave an insight into Moscow's eastward expansion and Siberian colonization—a sub-

The Eighteenth Century

proved unsuccessful, he at least gave impetus to others and served to presage a more enlightened method in the writing of history.

Müller (1705–1783).—Still greater service was performed by Gerhard Friedrich Müller, a phenomenally prodigious worker, in opening up to students of Russian history forgotten or unsuspected archival wealth.[9] A successor of Bayer,[10] one of the first German historians to settle in St. Petersburg, Müller emulated Bayer's diligence and his loyalty to historical knowledge, but not his erudition. "I do not demand," he wrote on one occasion, "that the historian must narrate everything he knows, nor even everything that is genuine, for there are things that could not be told or that are not interesting enough to be narrated to the public; but whatever the historian does state must be strictly true and never should he give any cause for suspicion to be directed toward himself."[11] He was only twenty when he arrived in the Russian capital from Leipzig, and, having no definite occupation, he decided to join Behring's expedition to Siberia. The trip, to Müller a mere escape from material difficulties, proved of such consequence as eventually to place him among the notable pioneers in the field of historical research in his adopted country. Müller was not a scholar, but a first-rank compiler—a fact for which we can be grateful, for no ambitious writer could ever have performed the valuable work which he did. With typical German diligence and persistence, he set out to copy voluminous collections of government records in the distant towns of Siberia. Ten years of fruitful labor (1733–1743) resulted in his being able to hand over to the Archeographical

4 *Modern Russian Historiography*

so much the early history of the Republic of Novgorod. While on a diplomatic mission to Sweden, he had met many scholars of that country, authorities on the early relations between Sweden and Novgorod.[4] Unfortunately, his work was handicapped by his preoccupation with politics, his utter lack of literary style, and an ignorance of Greek and Latin which prevented him from personally familiarizing himself with important sources both in Russia and abroad.

However, in 1739, after twenty years of laborious work, Tatishchev completed his ambitious undertaking and presented it to the Academy of Sciences for publication.[5] The manuscript was a bulky compilation of material, poorly digested and uncritical. It was looked at askance and severely censured because of its enormous size, the interpretation that it presented, and its defects in style.[6] The author was forced to revise it to suit the tastes of the members of the Academy, which was dominated by German scholars, but death prevented his completing the revision. Later, the manuscript was destroyed by fire. It was reproduced from copies in the possession of his colleagues, and thus, thanks particularly to Gerhard Friedrich Müller, the work of Tatishchev was saved from complete loss.[7] Notwithstanding well-deserved criticism, Tatishchev was one of the first historians in Russia with a vision broad enough to realize the relationships existing among the various factors which go to produce national life, and to comprehend that by understanding them one can construct a narrative of the nation's past as well as a historical philosophy. He saw the relation of history to other sciences—geography, ethnography, and economics.[8] If his attempt

The Eighteenth Century

of the age of Peter the Great, and an ardent admirer of the reforms of the Emperor, Tatishchev naturally turned westward—not to forsake the past, but to understand it more rationally. Under the direct encouragement of Peter himself, he set out to demonstrate to the Western world that Russia, too, had a history of which she might well be proud. Like most men of his time, Tatishchev began his career in the army. Later, as a product of the Petrine epoch, he became a mining engineer, and in this capacity he was on several occasions commissioned to go to western Europe, where he had an opportunity to observe closely the economic and political life of various nations. Still later, he held a number of responsible government positions in the Ural district, and for three years (1741–1744) was governor of Astrakhan Province.[2]

To Tatishchev history was a sort of by-product; his main interest was the economic development of national resources. But in pursuing his studies on this subject, he came to realize the utilitarian advantage of historical knowledge in general.[3] Moreover, his acquaintance with the national resources of his country revealed to him a wealth of archival material, and he began to collect sources from various parts of the vast Empire and from abroad, where he employed special copyists. His final aim was not merely to compile, but also to master the sources thoroughly and exhaustively, and to write an interpretative history; he realized full well the importance of a philosophy of history as opposed to a mere listing of events. His great ambition was to free Russian history from the current Germanic interpretation, particularly concerning the origin of the Slavs. It was for this reason that he emphasized national self-realization. Utilitarian in his view, he tried to link his own time with early periods and to derive practical lessons therefrom. Logical and level-headed, he maintained that historical interpretation should be based only on authentic sources. Schlözer, who with characteristic snobbery had little respect for Russian historians, made a single exception of Boltin, considering him the only native historian worth mentioning. Boltin, however, notwithstanding his original mind and intellectual foresight, failed to appreciate the gravest of all the problems of his time, serfdom. He thought that emancipation would be dangerous and certain to lead to disaster for the peasants and to economic calamity for the state.[29]

Summary

With Shcherbatov and Boltin, eighteenth-century Russian historiography comes to an end. None of the eighteenth-century historians had accomplished any critical study. Schlözer failed because of his total ignorance of the nature of Müller's collection; his only work worth noticing is his annotated edition of the *Chronicle of Nestor*.[30] As to the documents which Müller had begun to compile, they remained almost untouched. Shcherbatov and Boltin were aware of them, and Shcherbatov barely scratched their surface. The national archives were still a *terra incognita* to almost all the historians, partly because of the immense difficulty of early investigation, but chiefly because the government refused to open them to students of history.

Müller's services to Russian historiography can hardly be overestimated. His work of collecting did not permit him to do the historical writing he had hoped to do. His ambitious undertaking of the *Sammlung russischer Geschichte,* previously referred to, his *Monthly Publications* from 1755 to 1764 (twenty volumes, in Russian), and later his attempt to write a history of modern Russia, which received such a powerful rebuke from Lomonosov, achieved little except the stimulation of others to the writing of history.[31] With his appointment as archivist, he had to abandon editorial work completely and give all his attention to the tedious labor of investigating the hitherto unexplored national archives for the benefit of later students in this field. It is particularly worth noticing that Müller's search through the archives made possible a great and important task, yet one formerly impossible, the modern study of the history of Russia.

The chief link between the two centuries is the increasing search through the last decades of the eighteenth and the first of the nineteenth for documentary evidence upon which to construct a national history revealing a better understanding of the past and indicating a more intelligent course toward the future. Gradually the historian began to free himself from purely patriotic conceptions and to adopt the attitude described by Schlözer: a resistance to all patriotic motives, national, religious, or political, and an insistence upon the scholar's freedom to pursue, with undivided allegiance, nothing but historical truth. Slowly, Russian historical thought began to free itself from the religious interpretation borrowed from the chronicles, the utilitarianism of Tatishchev, and the panegyristic tendencies of Lomonosov. Tatishchev was already disinclined to include miracles in his history; Boltin denounced all historical writing that was not supported by authentic documentary evidence and handled in a scholarly manner; and the so-called German school—Müller, Schlözer, and Bayer—insisted upon objective national or universal history. These, briefly, constitute the intellectual legacy bequeathed to us by eighteenth-century Russian historiographers.

THE NINETEENTH CENTURY AND LATER

PUBLICATION OF SOURCES

THE PIONEERING WORK of the eighteenth century facilitated first of all the tremendous task of publishing the chronicles and other newly available source material that came to the knowledge of students of history. Schlözer's publication of *Nestor* aroused the interest of the government, and in 1804 Alexander I ordered the formation, at one of the universities in the Empire, of a society for the advancement of historical knowledge. The honor was bestowed upon the University of Moscow, and thus there came into being the first Russian historical society, the Moscow Society of History and Russian Antiquities.[32] This body set for its immediate goal the publication of the chronicles—the *Chronicle of Nestor* first, to be followed by all the others. Whatever may be thought of the early activities of the Moscow Society, and despite the reverses it met, one accomplishment cannot be overlooked: the intensive search by individual members for new sources and the publication of these new documents as begun by the Society. Among these papers were valuable chronicles, some of which aided Karamzin in his later writings. Furthermore, the activities of the Society roused Moscow's ancient rival, St. Petersburg, and a similar society was formed there. The rivalry between the two capitals and the accumulation of experience soon resulted in visible offshoots. Coincident with the activities of these emerging historical societies was the appearance of a veritable Maecenas, the distinguished Count Nikolay Petrovich Rumyantsev. This nobleman realized that before undertaking the writing of a general history the historian must have a thorough command of all the sources.[33] So it came about that the collective efforts of the Moscow Society and the feverish activity of a dilettante drove a deep furrow in the field of historical research. As State Chancellor and head of the Foreign Office, Count Rumyantsev was in a position to avail himself of every opportunity, and he missed none. A man of wealth, he could afford to purchase many rarities—which began to go up in price as the demand increased. The Moscow Society having been entrusted with the publication of the chronicles, Rumyantsev determined to publish, at his own expense, the diplomatic sources, and he spared neither money nor effort to make the edition a most luxurious one. For the publication of the *Collection of State Charters and Treaties* we owe him much.[34]

Rumyantsev was well aware that state charters and treaties alone would be insufficient, and that without the chronicles little progress could be made. Referring to these documents, he asked, "Is it believable that one of the greatest nations of the enlightened world and the single possessor of a treasure so significant not only for that nation, but also for all the persons occupied with history—is it believable that this nation, which ought to be proud of its past, should not hasten to announce and elaborate it to the world?"[35] He therefore lavishly supported the idea of publishing a complete collection of chronicles, donating altogether forty thousand rubles for this purpose.[36] Like many of his contemporaries, he was interested in the origins of the Russian people; unlike others, however, he looked much deeper into the past, including in it the growth of Arabian trade and the history of both the Near East and the Byzantine Empire. The ultimate key to early Russian history he hoped to trace not only in his own country, but abroad as well, and for this reason he sought the assistance of many foreign authorities in Byzantine and Oriental history. For the same purpose he dispatched a number of men to Germany, Italy, England, and Poland to investigate the archives of these countries and copy from them all the important documents relating to Russia.[37] In a word, Rumyantsev saw to it that every document bearing a relation to Russia's past found its place in the collection he intended to publish.[38] "The fuller and better this collection appears," he wrote to one of his assistants, "the more it will bring honor to you and pleasure in executing this enterprise to me. And whatever sums the expenses of its publication may require, I am ready to make sacrifices to supply them...."[39] Rumyantsev remained loyal to his promise, contributing his time, especially after his retirement from office in 1812, his money, and his energy. As a collector of sources for later historians, and the person financially responsible for their publication, he occupies a prominent place in the story of Russian historical research.[40]

In May, 1828, the Academy of Sciences voted ten thousand rubles to be sent to one of its ablest archivists, P. M. Stroyev, the head of the Archeographical Expedition to search through the vast empire for new source material. The story of this expedition is a dramatic tale in itself, with a record its chief could justly be proud of: more than two hundred libraries and various archives were searched and about three thousand documents copied.[41] The quantity of valuable material unearthed compelled the government to pursue the work further, and in December, 1834, the Ministry of Education was instructed to form an Archeographical Commission to be placed in charge of the publication of Stroyev's material. This task was successfully carried out in 1836, and a year later the Commission was made permanent. It led an independent life until 1922, when by a government decree it became a division of the Academy of Sciences of the Union of Socialist Soviet Republics.

In this long stretch of years the Archeographical Commission amassed a stupendous quantity of sources of all kinds. To mention only some of them: the Commission published four volumes of material provided by the Archeographical Expedition; a collection of the Russian chronicles in twenty-five volumes (to date); four volumes of legal documents (*Akty yuridicheskiye* and *Akty otnosyashchiesya do yuridicheskogo byta drevney Rossii*); the first five volumes of *Historical Documents* (*Akty istoricheskiye*), which are to be followed eventually by twelve supplementary volumes. Simultaneously, it edited twenty volumes of sources concerning western and southern Russia, three volumes of documents found in foreign archives, and thirty-seven volumes of various official papers (*Russkaya istoricheskaya biblioteka*), as well as numerous other collections. Also interesting is the fact that similar organizations soon sprang up elsewhere, notably at Kiev, Tiflis, and Vilna.[42] The government itself undertook the publication, in ten volumes, of all diplomatic material of the Muscovy period, and of the complete collection of laws, beginning with 1649, which became one of the principal sources of historical information for subsequent scholars. Such was the gigantic depository opened to Russian students by the second half of the nineteenth century. Karamzin was the first to benefit noticeably from the generosity of men like Rumyantsev and from the opportunity of having at his disposal voluminous papers formerly unknown or their existence only suspected.

Karamzin (1766-1826).—The typical successor of the eighteenth-century historians was Nikolay Mikhaylovich Karamzin, son of a Simbirsk landlord, whose education was begun at a private school in Moscow and continued at the university in the same city. Here he met the well-known liberal, Freemason, and distinguished publisher, N. I. Novikov, and another eminent Mason, I. P. Turgenev. From May, 1789, to September, 1790, Karamzin toured Europe, including England, and recorded his impressions in his widely read *Letters of a Russian Traveler*.[43] While abroad he observed closely the life of western Europe, chiefly from the point of view of a philosopher and literatus. His first impressions inclined him to a great admiration for Western civilization. England failed to arouse the enthusiasm of the "Russian traveler," and except for a warm appreciation of the Anglo-Saxon judicial genius he left the British Isles "as cold as the English themselves"; but Paris made an overwhelming impression upon him.[44] This city, the pulse of European political and social life, made him believe that the only solution for mankind lay in cosmopolitanism; that first of all one must be a man, and only second a Russian.[45] He became an admirer of Robespierre, whose premature death he deeply regretted. However, this outburst of poetic enthusiasm was only temporary. Later, he began to discard his cosmopolitan ideas, exchanging them for reactionary nationalism. The Napoleonic wars assisted in definitely completing his political convictions, best expressed in his famous Memorandum, *Old and New Russia,* presented to Alexander I in 1811: it proved that the author was *plus royaliste que le roi.*

Upon closer observation of the west, Karamzin evidently was hurt by the strikingly unfavorable contrast with his own country. Whether in self-defense or self-consolation, he adopted the attitude that Russia had her own glorious history and that she need not shrink before Europe; all she needed was a Russian Tacitus and a Michelangelo to demonstrate her greatness. Russia, wrote Karamzin in one of his letters from Paris, "had her own Charles the Great—Vladimir; her own Louis XI—Tsar Ivan III; her own Cromwell—Godunov," and such an emperor as Peter I western Europe had never seen.[46] The rôle of a Russian Tacitus, Karamzin seems to have imposed upon himself some years later.

On his return to Russia, Karamzin continued to lead an easygoing life, occupying himself chiefly with literary writing—poetry and prose. As he began to advance in years his interest in history increased. His panegyrics to Catherine II and the famous ode dedicated to Alexander I on the occasion of Alexander's accession to the throne, as well as his frequent articles in the *Messenger of Europe,* a periodical edited by him, made him popular at court. He had already demonstrated his reverence of monarchy in his essay on Catherine II written in 1801, glorifying the memory of the Empress, who, he said, had taught Russia how to reason and to love the virtue radiating from the purple robe.[47] In 1803 the state granted him the title of "Historiographer" and allowed him an annual pension of two thousand rubles, on condition that he write a complete history of Russia. The following year, he retired as editor of the *Messenger of Europe* and began to write his *History of the Russian State,* a work which gave him wide publicity and started the legend of his being the "first Russian historian."[48] This work appeared in 1816 in eight volumes; it was followed in 1821 by the ninth, and in 1824 by the tenth and eleventh volumes. In 1826 he died without completing the twelfth volume, which leads up to the seventeenth century.[49]

The title of Karamzin's history is revealing: it is a history of the Russian state, not of the Russian people. It is not even that: it is a rhetorical, panegyristic narrative which endeavors to prove that autocracy alone has bestowed all the blessings that the Russian Empire ever enjoyed; it is an album of sovereigns accompanied by a description in the most resounding style. The approach of the author to his subject encompassed, no doubt, a gigantic sweep, but he was badly handicapped by his "monarchical blinders." Besides, Karamzin began his history without proper training for such work; critical history was totally alien to him. His contemporaries, Schlözer or Niebuhr, had no influence whatever upon him. Being more a representative of sentimental romanticism in fiction than of scholarly historical writing, he was naturally inclined to consider history as in large part a beautiful narrative, in which the characters were either heroes to be worshiped or vicious men to be deplored; the masses did not count; everything emanated from a single source—strong government; and justice "radiated from the purple robe." He still believed that the seemingly empty past of Russia could be made into a beautiful tale. All one must possess, to cite Karamzin's own words, is "mind, taste, and talent"; then he could "select, inspirit, and illuminate, and the reader would be amazed to see how, for instance, a Chronicle of Nestor could be transformed into something attractive, powerful, worthy of the attention not only of Russians, but also of foreigners."[50] With such aims and a generous pension, Karamzin could give free rein to his artistic pen, his poetic imagination, and his political bias.

According to Karamzin, early Kievan Russia reached a high degree of development because of its strong monarchical government. The downfall of old Russia is explained by the peculiarly established political custom of dividing the state among the royal heirs. This was corrected by the rise of a strong state in the north, Moscow, which not only freed Russia from the Tartars but also united it into a powerful nation. It is the traditional "Great Russian" interpretation, the theory that the entire historical process was centrifugal rather than centripetal—a theory later to be vehemently opposed by Hrushevsky.

In justice to Karamzin, it must be stated that his *History* is not without some merit, in spite of its pontifical presentation. His florid literary style tended to liberate Russian historical writing from the antiquated church-Slavonic terminology so greatly admired by members of the old school and to introduce a more eloquent, vigorous, even though rhetorical, style that appealed to literary aesthetes of his time.[51] Furthermore, his work stimulated an unprecedented interest in national history;[52] to Pushkin, Karamzin was "the Columbus of Russian History." Finally, many of the footnotes refer to or contain citations from valuable sources which were destroyed in the Moscow fire of 1812 and are thus not available to present-day students; Karamzin's private library was destroyed, and so were other private and official archives. (Altogether, Karamzin's *History* contains 6538 references, truly a history in itself!) The nature of the documents destroyed is known to us only through the references of Karamzin.[53]

Despite these merits, his work is now a mere curiosity rather than a study. It totally lacks historical perspective, since Karamzin could not conceive of a historical process; like the eighteenth-century rationalist, he saw in history only evil or benevolent sovereigns who led the country either to disaster or to glory. It is very doubtful whether Karamzin could have examined sufficiently the sources to which he refers in his footnotes, though the archives were at his disposal and he was generously aided by high officials and friends, among them M. Muravyev, the Assistant Minister of Education, Count N. Rumyantsev, A. Malinovsky, head of the Archives, and his close friend, A. I. Turgenev, who gathered and copied documents for him abroad, particularly at the papal archives. It was a physical impossibility within the comparatively short period of time, interrupted by frequent illnesses, for him to go over the voluminous amount of material referred to; and though he never mentions them, he relied in great part upon references cited in secondary authorities, thereby creating an impression of extraordinary erudition.[54]

Of the secondary authorities which greatly aided Karamzin, there must be mentioned Schlözer's edition of the *Chronicle of Nestor,* for the earlier period of Russian history, and Shcherbatov's for the later. Shcherbatov's history was not only a ready pattern for the literary embroidery of Karamzin, but also the best guide to the sources. Professor Milyukov, by comparing page after page, has shown how closely Karamzin followed the general outline of Shcherbatov.[55] To Shcherbatov's bulky work all Karamzin had to add was literary style and poetic imagination, exactly the qualities Prince Shcherbatov had lacked, and history would indeed become well "selected, inspirited, and illuminated." A single citation from Karamzin, describing the eve of the historical battle of Kulikov of September 8, 1380, will prove better than any lengthy discourse the truth of this statement:[56]

The noise of arms had not quieted down in the town and the people looked with emotion at the brave warriors ready to die for the Fatherland and Faith. It seemed as if the Russian people had awakened after a deep sleep: the long terror of the Tartars had vanished from their hearts as if removed by some supernatural power. They reminded one another of the glorious Vozhsk battle; they enumerated all the evils they had suffered from the barbarians during the hundred and fifty years and wondered at the shameful patience of their forefathers. Princes, boyars, townsmen, peasants, all were fired with equal enthusiasm, for the tyranny of the Khans oppressed all equally, from the throne to the hut. What was more just than the sword at such a noble and unanimous call?

Patriotic? To this accusation Karamzin's disarming reply was that where there is no love there is no soul. He never shrank before such criticism. "I know that I need the impartiality of a historian; forgive me, but I was not always able to conceal my love toward the Fatherland."[57] It was this very "soul" that made his history so popular; the first edition of three thousand sets at the prohibitive price of fifty-five rubles a set was sold out within twenty-five days.[58] But the very reasons which made Karamzin's history popular discredited it with the critical scholar.

Even in Karamzin's lifetime his work was under fire because of its bias and its antiquated interpretation of the past.[59] The criticism came mainly from the Westerners, or "skeptics" as they were called in Russian historiography, who were under the influence chiefly of Schlözer and Niebuhr. Polevoy considered Karamzin's *History* an outdated piece of work before it was produced; Pogodin thought even the title of the twelve-volume work a mistake and the author to be as far from Gibbon as intellectual England was from Russia.[60] M. Kachenovsky, editor of the *Messenger of Europe,* wrote in 1818 a review in which he described it as nothing but insolence in the face of western Europe, "a chronicle masterfully written by an artist of superb talent, but not a history." The well-known Decembrist, Nikita Muravyev, disapproved of it on the grounds that "history belongs to the people and not

The Nineteenth Century and Later

the tsars," while a biting epigram, ascribed to Pushkin, dedicated to Karamzin four lines, which, translated, read:

> In his history, beauty and simplicity
> Prove without bias
> The necessity of autocracy
> And the charm of the knout.

But these were only isolated voices drowned by the general shouts of hosanna to the author; conservative Russia celebrated Karamzin as the first national historian, and his twelve-volume work remained for a long time the official history of Russia.

Polevoy (1796-1846).—Among the earlier successors of Karamzin who undertook the reinterpretation of Russian history was Nikolay Alekseyevich Polevoy. Born in Irkutsk as the son of a merchant, he was a typical self-made man and representative of the rising "classless intelligentsia." Though a journalist of high rank, he lacked the refinement of Karamzin.[61] He became an admirer of Guizot, Thierry, and particularly of Niebuhr, whose teachings inspired him to do historical writing. The title of Polevoy's work, *A History of the Russian People,* indicates the idea behind it. This work he dedicated to the historian he most greatly admired, Barthold Georg Niebuhr.[62] The aim of the author was to follow the school of western historians, to narrate without bias the past of his people, to show the part the Russian nation had played in the general historical drama of the western world; he did not aim to paint a mere gallery of tsars.[63] Moreover, Polevoy was not content with the humble rôle of a chronicler; to him history was a "practical revaluation of philosophical conceptions concerning the universe and mankind, an analysis of a philosophical synthesis." National history he therefore hoped to write not from a purely local point of view, but in the light of universal developments.[64] In this respect Polevoy was far ahead not only of his contemporaries, but even of his immediate successors. The task, however, proved much beyond his capacities. His work is a bold attempt, yet proves once more the inevitable futility of a noble ambition unaccompanied by adequate intellectual equipment.

Pogodin (1800–1875).—Among the first historians to rise against the "skeptics" was Mikhail Petrovich Pogodin.[65] Like Polevoy, Pogodin was descended from a humble family; his father was a serf, belonging to Count Stroganov. But, living in Moscow, the boy somehow came into contact with university life, and after being graduated he joined the faculty. Both Karamzin and Schlözer were great favorites of his, though, strictly speaking, he was a follower of neither. He worked out his own method of writing, but the reactionary era through which he lived stamped its imprint upon his work.

Like many of his contemporaries, Pogodin was interested in early Russian history, and especially in the Varangian problem, a topic which he ably developed in his *Annals of Nestor*. His master's dissertation, *Concerning the Origins of Russia*, written in 1824, was highly praised by Karamzin and opened to the author the doors of his alma mater.[66] Yet, when he applied for permission to go abroad, the government refused him the privilege, announcing that "present circumstances make it useless to send this master to foreign lands to complete his studies, for it is more convenient to give him in the university that kind of education which the government would consider profitable."[67]

Pogodin's *History of Russia* is a remarkable piece of work; in it he reveals an amazing knowledge of all the Russian sources available at that time. An enormously detailed study, it sadly lacks, however, a synthetic grasp. This is not surprising, in view of the nationalistic ideas of the author and his lack of foreign travel. It is therefore better described as a voluminous source book than as a history.

Two forces, Pogodin maintained, assisted in the formation of the Russian state: Greek or Byzantine Christianity from the south, and Slavic learning from the southwest. Russia being strong in the possession of these two mighty streams, Pogodin did not fear, as did others, to acknowledge the existence of Germanic influence, or what was known as the "Norman period" in early Russian history. The foundation laid by the Normans, he insisted, was unstable and had therefore been easily overthrown by the Tartars; only with the rise of Moscow came the true national state, which received its final expression in Peter the Great. Much of his interpretation was borrowed from Schlözer, but he added a strong national color to the general picture of the past. Pogodin's reverence for Nestor is most characteristic; he urged the Russian people to "proclaim his eternal memory and to worship him so that he may grant us the spirit of Russian history, for the spirit alone, my friends, uplifts, while the letter alone kills...." Such lines could have been written only by a native Russian, not by a German academician.[68]

Pogodin, though he received a broader education than Polevoy, set sail on shallower waters. In 1835 he was appointed Professor of Russian History in the University of Moscow, taking the place of his former teacher, Kachenovsky. The appointment was well fitted to the general policy of the current administration, for Pogodin had no sympathy with the beliefs of the "skeptics" concerning a "universal philosophical synthesis"; and anything even remotely related to "universality" was considered at that time a menace to autocracy and orthodoxy. Pogodin's reverence for Russian antiquities in the strictest orthodox sense could not but meet with the approval of the administration of Nicholas I. As lecturer in the University of Moscow and editor of the *Moscow Messenger* (1827-1830) and later of the *Moskvityanin* (1841-1856), he followed an extremely nationalistic course. How one could embrace both the broad principles of Schlözer and a homespun patriotism was a mystery even to his contemporaries, but that was the mystery, also, of his time.[69] Did not even Polevoy, crushed by many reverses, become, according to Herzen, "within five days a loyal subject"? The duality of Pogodin gave sufficient ground for both the Westerners and the Slavophiles to claim him as the advocate of the ideas of each.

The Westerners and Slavophiles.—"Westernism" and "Slavophilism" constitute a complex phenomenon, to which I shall refer only so far as the immediate subject is concerned. The policy of isolating Russia from a contagious western Europe, which Nicholas I followed, gave impetus to the crystallization of vague discussions of Russian history, and resulted in a sharper demarcation between the two segments of thought known as the Western and the Slavophile schools. These two schools diverged widely in their interpretation of Russian history, and a literary war was declared along the entire front. Chaadayev's famous *Philosophical Letter,* which appeared in 1836, was the opening gun.[70] The tenseness of the struggle led to extreme theories, often totally unsound. The pessimist Peter Chaadayev saw only three stages in the past of his country: "at first savage barbarism, then primitive superstition, and later brutal, humiliating foreign oppression, the qualities of which were afterward inherited by the national government."[71] The Westerners of the 'forties did not view Russian history with such pessimism—not, at any rate, under the influence of Catholic Romanticism, as Chaadayev did,—yet there was a streak of similarity in their negation of the past. They, too, rejected the old Russia, but they thought that Russia must find her salvation not in the mystical, religious western world, but in following the political road toward the emancipation of the masses, achieved long before in Europe. Their concept of a higher stage of development was that of a parliamentary form of government on a western model. To many of them the state remained supreme, and all else was subordinated to its unquestionable sovereignty.

The Slavophiles and Westerners differed widely in their opinions concerning the reforms of Peter I. The Westerners considered the period of Peter to be the starting point of modern Russia, the Russian Renaissance. They rejected the arguments of the Slavophiles that these reforms violated the course of national evolution, and branded this philosophy as homespun patriotism which only aided in maintaining Oriental despotism. This opinion naturally offended many ardent nationalists, who, with sentimental naïveté, in self-defense developed their own philosophy—in which, however, they assumed equally erroneous theories. Such was, for example, the theory of the extreme Slavophile leaders who believed that Russian civilization was far superior to western; that Russia was a world in itself to which western yardsticks were not applicable;* and, finally, that Russia was strong because of the stability of her social and political institutions. The Slavophiles considered the reforms of Peter I as a fatal blunder, since they thrust upon the country a philo-European monarchy, antinational laws, and customs to which the people would never consent. They praised the system of communal landownership, which, they said, protected the peasants from poverty and prevented the rise of the socially restless element, the urban proletariat. The Slavophiles therefore urged the preservation of all institutions associated with the ancient customs of the nation, and did not favor the forcing of alien ideas upon a people which had its own rich past.

Without making a detailed study of the two schools, it may be noted that the resulting antagonism not only aided in producing liberals like Herzen, critics like Belinsky, teachers like Granovsky, and writers and publicists like Samarin, Valuyev, Khomyakov, the Kireyevsky brothers, and Aksakov, but also contributed significantly to the development

---

* Compare this view with that of the later Eurasian school, discussed elsewhere; and see D. S. Mirsky, "The Eurasian Movement," *Slavonic Review*, December, 1927, 314, 315–316.

of history. The tenseness awakened an unprecedented interest in ethnography, in Russian folklore, and especially in Russian history since each camp sought in that subject the revelation of universal reason upon which to build its philosophy.[72] Seizing upon the ideas of Hegel and Schelling concerning the successive ascent of nations with historic missions for mankind, they tried to find justification for their hopes that the next message to the world would be given by Russia.

Those who took sides in this dispute—and it was difficult to remain neutral—turned not only to the national history but to western European history as well. Young men grew absorbed in the writings of the French Encyclopedists, were fascinated with the philosophies of Kant, Fichte, Schelling, and, most of all, Hegel, who became the idol of a whole generation. The intellectual fever of the middle of the nineteenth century brought forth in Russia a series of brilliant scholars, whose names, with a few exceptions, alas, mean little to western readers. Suffice it to mention Aksakov, Zabelin, or I. Belyayev, the last named being known for his investigations of earlier periods of Moscow life, chiefly concerning the peasant problem, communal landownership, and conditions of the Slavic tribes before the coming of the Varangians; or Kavelin and Dmitriyev, later to be followed by that prolific scholar, A. Pypin, noted for his studies in recent Russian political and social history, Russian Freemasonry, and Slavic literature; or V. Sergeyevich, the distinguished student of legal history, whose *Antiquities of Russian Law* remains to this day a monument to scholarship; or B. Chicherin, Hegelian, eminent jurist, and philosopher, whose chief contribution was in the field of Russian local government of the eighteenth century. The list could be greatly lengthened, but the limited scope of this study does not permit a detailed account of this period of "storm and stress" in Russian history. Since this survey can include only the pillars of modern historiography, produced by the intellectual fermentation of the time, I shall now consider the most imposing of them, namely, Solovyev.

Solovyev (1820–1879).—Sergey Mikhaylovich Solovyev came at a time when Russian historiography was in need of a writer who could amalgamate all the divergent theories accumulated through preceding decades into a single work. This was a task too great for any one man; but Solovyev assumed it and carried it an almost unbelievable distance. Solovyev was born in Moscow and until he was fourteen years old received his education at home. His father was a priest and teacher from whom the young son inherited a profound religious faith, which later colored strongly his outlook upon history. In 1838 he entered the University of Moscow, where he was a pupil of both Pogodin and Granovsky. He fell especially under the influence of Granovsky, and for the rest of his life was closely attached to him. Granovsky's synthetic interpretation of history at once arrested his attention. Like many young people of his day, Solovyev had to sail toward intellectual maturity between the Scylla and Charybdis of Westernism and Slavophilism. For a time he leaned toward Slavophilism, until, by careful reading of Russian history, he was "cured." But the "cure" was evidently not thorough: Solovyev retained his faith in the religious and political Messianism of Russia and was a firm believer in the monarchical form of government, though he softened his theory by the amendment that the government should rule with the consent of the "better portions of the nation." Among the historians who determined the career of Solovyev was Ewers.* His work on early Russian history marked an epoch in Solovyev's intellectual life, "since Karamzin supplied only facts based on emotion," whereas Ewers forced him to do original thinking about Russian history.

During the years 1842-1844 Solovyev traveled abroad, as tutor in the family of Count Stroganov, and he made wise use of every available hour. In Paris he audited the lectures of Michelet, Victor Chasles, Edgar Quinet, and Lenormand, successor of Guizot; here he also made the acquaintance of the greatest of all poets of Poland, Adam Mickiewicz. In Prague he met the leading Czech philologist and Slavophile, Šafařík; and in Berlin he audited the lectures of August Neander. During his short sojourn in Europe he also familiarized himself with western historical literature. He returned to Russia with a warm reverence for Giovanni Vico as the great thinker of the eighteenth century and for Guizot as the eminent historian of his own time.[73] The breadth of Solovyev's interest is characteristic. Unlike many historians, especially of the later generation, he demonstrated an amazing knowledge of universal history. He was also excellently versed in European history and culture, in the broadest sense, and was a keen student of ancient civilizations.

---

* J. P. G. Ewers was a student of Schlözer at Göttingen. In 1803 Ewers came to Russia, and established there his permanent residence. His most important contributions are *Vom Ursprunge des russischen Staats* (1808) and *Das älteste Recht der Russen in seiner geschichtlichen Entwickelung* (1826).

Upon his return from Europe, Solovyev was appointed to the faculty of the University of Moscow to teach Russian history, a chair held by his former teacher Pogodin, who had retired in 1844. As lecturer and writer, Solovyev stood forth as a determined opponent of "periods" in Russian history, whether "appanage" or any other. All "periods," he maintained, were wrong, misleading, and they obscured the organic unity of events. This new view was bound to leave indelible marks on the development of Russian historiography. Former historical writing, with its "epochs" loosely hanging in the air and artificially fitted side by side, had to be abandoned; the historian was compelled to embrace the past in its entirety, and only for convenience might he divide it into "stages of development." With such a design, Solovyev set out to rewrite history, and in 1851 there appeared the first volume of his famous *History of Russia*. In the next twenty-eight years there followed volume after volume, twenty-nine altogether, ending with the date 1774.[74] His original project was to lead up to the nineteenth century, which would have required at least six more volumes; death, interrupting the author in the middle of a sentence, prevented the completion of the plan.

In this voluminous work Solovyev attempted on an unprecedented scale not only to give a record of events, but also to explain those events, trace their origins, link their correlations, and derive sound conclusions. He soberly analyzed the social, economic, and political forces and the geographic environment which contributed to the changes in society, beginning with the time when ancient Slav tribes, who lived, as he thought, along the Danube, were forced eastward by some other people to a totally bare and inhospitable territory which was later to become known as Russia, leaving behind them the fertile and strategically more convenient lands. Scattered along the Dniester, Dnieper, and Oka rivers, they required a long time for readjustment, while constant invasions of Asiatic hordes from the east and bitter rivalry with Poland and Lithuania along the western frontiers made progress virtually impossible. Herein lay the main reason for Russia's backwardness. The more favorable geographic position of the Muscovite principality aided its political growth. Being farther away from immediate danger and exploiting every occasion for consolidating its powers at the expense of its weaker neighbors, this principality gradually laid the foundation for the future Moscow state, upon which, later, was to arise the Russian Empire.[75]

His thesis concerning the rise of the Russian state, Solovyev developed somewhat as follows. State and nation, he explained, are inseparable, the one deriving from the other; the history of Russia is a history of its government. This view, obviously, shows very strongly the influence of Hegel and Ranke. In the presence of this broad conception and the remarkable logic of Solovyev, the works of the earlier writers become definitely superseded.

It was the first time that a history of Russia had been conceived on such a scale, with the narrative based always on the authentic source and held fast to the principle of pure, objective truth. In this comprehensive conception both of history and of the nation in all the aspects of its life, Solovyev emphasized three main factors—political, religious, and cultural, and found their expression in "loyalty to the State, devotion to the Church, and struggle for enlightenment." His emphasis upon cultural development was in harmony with the practice of the historians of the western nations, so that his development of Russia's history against a background that ranged beyond mere national limitations brought him closer to the Westerners. At the same time his broad knowledge of his subject and his strictly critical approach to every problem in his work won respect even among those who could not agree with his view. Solovyev, however, considered the work to which he had devoted half his life as only a tool to be used in clearing the way for a closer, fuller, and perhaps more philosophical study of Russian development.[76]

Solovyev's entire work is based exclusively on archival material, most of which was new. It should be considered, indeed, as an encyclopedia of the nation's growth rather than a mere history. In this fact lies its merit as well as its weakness. One of its shortcomings is that, notwithstanding the author's insistence upon "organic unity," his twenty-nine volumes constitute an Everest of historical material mounted with Hegelian design but lacking any proper integration. In this respect Solovyev was right when he described his work as only a tool for later scholars; and it still offers sufficient raw material to be often well worth consulting. Solovyev did not possess a speculative mind; whatever was obscure he omitted, and he never indulged in hypothetical interpretations. This is the main reason, says Klyuchevsky, why Solovyev's history contains so little "learned trash," and may explain also why the author has been labeled a "dry historian."[77] Solovyev had neither the literary gift of Klyuchevsky nor time to be concerned about style or beauty; he was occupied with "pick and shovel" work; otherwise, how could he have produced a twenty-nine-volume history, not to mention many other works? He left a mass of raw material with numerous threads hanging at loose ends. It became the task of his pupil and successor, Klyuchevsky, to weave these threads together into a beautiful design, embodying in historical writing of supreme excellence a summary of all the efforts of all the Russian historians, beginning with Tatishchev in the eighteenth century. But before we examine the work of Klyuchevsky, we must consider that of Kavelin.

Kavelin (1818-1885).—The German school of Ranke, Niebuhr, Eichhorn, and Savigny found in Russia many strong disciples other than Solovyev. A contemporary of Solovyev and a pupil of the same school was Konstantine Dmitrievich Kavelin, who, very much as Solovyev had done, endeavored to apply to his own country the German philosophy of history, namely, that national development represents an organic process based on immutable laws which neither the individual genius nor historical incidents can offset.[78] Not the genius of the leader but the genius of the people ultimately shapes the destiny of a nation; and, very much as the *Iliad* and the *Odyssey* represent products of the collective genius of the Greek people, so is social life the product of the collective will or genius rather than of the will or genius of a single member, preëminent though he may be. Kavelin stressed little the economic or cultural aspects of social life and dwelt more upon those "immutable laws" which controlled the historical procession of changes that a society was bound to undergo.[79] The fundamental law of history, Kavelin believed, is the organic growth and transformation of the community from a tribal condition into a modern state. This process naturally has ramifications, but historical law prescribes the final goal toward which the group blindly moves; resistance to this law explains the civil strife which has occurred from time to time in the past. It was in accord with this law that Kavelin conceived the rise of the Muscovite state. Whereas Solovyev believed that the centralized Russian state had evolved in large part because of a number of favorable historical coincidences, Kavelin denied such an assumption, insisting that a state had to emerge as a historical inevitability since a society was bound to undergo certain prescribed stages in its development "from the tribal stage with its common form of ownership to the family with its heritable estate or separate ownership, to the person and the state."[80]

Kavelin's interpretation seemed too rigid, too dogmatic to many students, among whom were the Slavophiles, who felt that this theory upset their philosophy that the peasant commune was a far superior social form than the supposedly higher stage of individual ownership. Another group was represented by Chicherin and Sergeyevich, who maintained that the state came into being not because of historical laws but by virtue of civil contracts. Sergeyevich saw two main stages in the development of the state: the first, when the individual will was supreme; the second, when the sovereignty of the state absorbed the individual will. Later came

Klyuchevsky and Kostomarov, the first approaching the problem with an eye mainly upon its social-economic aspects, the second, upon its ethnographic, thus leaving very little of the laboriously erected theory of Kavelin. But the destruction of the various philosophical theories stimulated historical thought, sharpened the intellect of men, and tempered their will to know, to understand, and to expound their principles; and this, to a nation culturally alive, is worth more than belief in a static "eternal truth."

The "Great Reforms" of the 'sixties stimulated greatly the study of law and institutions in Russia. This was the period which subsequently produced a legion of scholars, among whom were such eminent students as Gradovsky, Korkunov, Sergeyevich, Latkin, Dyakonov, Filippov, Romanovich-Slavatinsky, and Nolde, who investigated Russian institutions; others, like Vladimirsky-Budanov, who made a comparative study of Russian and western public law and institutions; and a third group, Lappo and Lyubavsky, who concentrated upon Lithuanian history. The towering figure among all these writers was Gradovsky, who studied thoroughly the political institutions in western Europe and came to admire the principles of legality and political liberty.[81] To him history was mainly a matter of legal development, and with this view he set out to present Russia's past with an emphasis upon the rôle of national and local institutions in the growth of the nation, their interrelationships and their conflicts. As professor at the University of St. Petersburg, he left a whole school of disciples, known in Russia as the "historico-juridical school" since it interpreted the state as "a juridical relation, the subject of which is all the [capable] population, and the object—the power of domination." Some of these men became world-renowned authorities, like N. Tagantsev in the field of criminal law, and F. Martens in international law.*

Klyuchevsky (1841-1911).—Vasily Osipovich Klyuchevsky was born in the Province of Penza in the family of a village priest. His early years brought him close to peasant life, an experience that later enabled him to view the vital agrarian problem and the origins of serfdom not only with rare sympathy but also with remarkable insight and intuition, qualities quite alien to court panegyrists and city-bred intelligentsia. In 1856 Klyuchevsky entered an ecclesiastical seminary. He made an excellent record there, but after four years he determined to follow a different path. The seminary board was reluctant to grant him a leave, insisting that he was receiving a government stipend and was therefore under moral obligation to pursue the career he had chosen; but the bishop looked at the matter differently, and Klyuchevsky was permitted to leave. The following year he enrolled in the University of Moscow. It was the year of the great reforms, and many youths were fired with the hope of a brighter day for their country. Klyuchevsky plunged into the midst of this feverish period—a turning point in modern Russia—with the utmost interest for everything that concerned the national life.

At the University Klyuchevsky was fortunate in finding still there the "old guard," among them G. Ivanov, the stimulating lecturer on ancient civilizations, and S. Solovyev, the

---

* A critical appraisal of the juridical school is ably presented by N. Milyukov in his brief article, "Yuridicheskaya shkola v russkoy istoriografii: Solovyev, Kavelin, Chicherin, Sergeyevich," *Russkaya mysl'*, VI (1886), 80-92.

great historian. Solovyev was then in the prime of his popularity, and he deeply impressed the young man. It is from Solovyev, his greatly admired teacher, that Klyuchevsky received his broad vision of history, learned the necessity of a mastery of sources, and gained a sense of purpose in the historical process that did not permit of an aimless flow of events. His early study based on the accounts of foreign travelers concerning the Muscovite state won immediate attention, and at Solovyev's suggestion he undertook a number of other studies. Chief among them was his master's dissertation on the lives of the Russian saints as a historical source. Another study dealt with the Solovetsky monastery as a factor in the economic development of the north, and further confirmed the expectations of the teacher.[82] But Klyuchevsky's ambition was not attracted to local developments however important; he wanted to paint a broad design on a national scale. Endowed with the vision and the temperament of the artist, only self-discipline and determination enabled him to complete a study based on boring accounts of an old monastery. But the tedious work was not wasted; it developed in Klyuchevsky qualities indispensable for the historian—patience, and a keen analytical ability which he employed to scrutinize the numerous sources—sifting much sand for a few grains of gold—as well as to take full advantage of his access to source material never before examined. It also enabled him to familiarize himself with a field rarely dwelt upon in a scholarly manner—the relation between church and state, and the part played by the church in the economic development of the Russian people.

Klyuchevsky's lectures on Russian history at the Alexandrian military school and at the University of Moscow for Women demonstrated not only his exceptional ability as a lecturer, but also his rare literary gift and his remarkable vision and talent in imparting a glowing, vivid reality to dusty archival records. Within a few years he had become widely known, and when, in 1879, Solovyev became gravely ill, Klyuchevsky was given the chair of his teacher. Many students at the University of Moscow looked askance at the young appointee, the teacher from a military school and a women's university! Speedily, however, as one of his pupils recalls,[83] his lectures became so popular that it was futile to offer anything else in the hours when Klyuchevsky lectured: he would empty all other auditoriums.

Klyuchevsky is especially noteworthy for his remarkable grasp of the scope of the historical process and for the richness of his cultural knowledge. He was an active member of the Moscow Archeological Society. In 1900 he consented, after continuous and persistent pressure, to lecture at the School of Fine Arts, and there he remained to his closing days. His addresses on Pushkin, Lermontov, and Fonvizin, later published in the form of essays, bear witness to his profound knowledge of literature;[84] and his *Course in Russian History,* delivered at the University of Moscow, reveals an amazing genius for presenting synthetic history, and stands today a monument to Russian letters. For a long time Klyuchevsky's lectures were known only through the notes of students. All attempts to persuade him to publish them in book form met with his disapproval because he felt that they were far from being the last word on Russian history.[85] He finally yielded, however, and in 1904 there appeared the first volume of his popular *Course,* which was soon followed by three more; in 1921 there appeared a fifth volume, compiled from the notes of a former student, Y. Barskov.[86]

Klyuchevsky came at a time when Slavophilism, Westernism, and Hegelianism were beginning to fade; the old feudal order was definitely passing away, and everywhere there were signs of the emergence of a new Russia. Thus Klyuchevsky was in the advantageous position of one who could look back at times and at schools which had flourished and gone; and he made the best of his opportunity. In his work he considered the past ten centuries of Russia horizontally: at the bottom, the "dark" peasant masses; at the top, the gentry nurtured physically by the masses and intellectually by French culture; between these, the other classes, dependent on both. These social layers were now antagonistic, now allied, as circumstances dictated. Throughout the entire process of social formation run certain concrete factors: struggle for national unity, the demands of national defense, the longing for cultural development, and the desire for economic security.[87] These factors make his narrative systematic, unique, and purposeful. The only criticism one can make is that the author gave too little space to Russian foreign policy, emphasizing mainly the internal development of the Empire; the Foreign Office occupies no place of prominence in Klyuchevsky's history.

Klyuchevsky's approach to any past event was never that of the cold logician-scientist with lancet poised to probe, but rather that of the keen, sympathetically intuitive psychologist; yet never did his rich and fertile mind betray the scientific accuracy of his observations or his judgment. Therefore his generalizations are usually sound, his characters emerge from the distant past clothed in flesh and blood, and the whole process of historical development becomes a vivid, integrated panorama. His striking accomplishment is his harmonization within himself of the qualities of an erudite historian, a sociologist, an artist, and a teacher. As he turns the pages of Klyuchevsky's *Course,* how the episodes of the past are revived before the reader! How can one not marvel at the artist-historian who gives us such living portraits as those of Ivan the Terrible, Boris Godunov, Patriarch Nikon, or Peter the Great? Not alone the students of history learned from Klyuchevsky, but accomplished artists like Shalyapin as well.[88]

No previous Russian history had given so much space to the peasant problem. The peasant of Kievan Russia in all his multiple forms—the frontiersman, tradesman, and tiller of the soil, whether free or enslaved in field or factory, whether groaning under the burden of heavy taxes, submissive and downtrodden at the feet of his master, or great and terrible in the reawakened spirit of his frontier ancestors of the wide plains of Russia—this peasant finds paramount place in Klyuchevsky's history. For the historian realized that it is only by the systematic analysis of the peasant as well as the agrarian problem that Russian history will be fully appreciated.

Though Klyuchevsky greatly revered his teachers, Solovyev and Chicherin, he left them far behind.[89] Solovyev, like

Buckle, later emphasized the influence of "spiritual forces" upon history; his pupil turned more to the political, social, and economic. To him the forces of real importance were less the moral than the material forces, those which manifested themselves in social phenomena. And if to Chicherin institutions meant everything, to Klyuchevsky they were simply mechanical things shaped by the sociological process of a nation. Among the works that display this conception are the analytical study of the Council of Boyars, which remains to this day a classic piece of historical literature; the study of the value of the ruble from the sixteenth to the eighteenth century; and, finally, the essay on the origins of serfdom, a reply to J. Engelmann's book, *Die Leibeigenschaft in Russland* [*The Institution of Serfdom in Russia*], in which the author endeavors to prove that peasant indebtedness was the main condition that led to the establishment of the institution of serfdom.[90] This essay presented a highly original view, though it is somewhat questioned by present-day scholars, who are inclined to attach more importance to direct state legislation than to any abstract process.

Klyuchevsky destroyed many of the happier notions of the past, notably those held by the Slavophiles. For instance, the Slavophiles were always fond of pointing out that in the earlier days Russia was governed by a limited monarch, the agency to limit his powers being the *Zemsky Sobor* (National Assembly). Klyuchevsky exploded that theory by proving that so far as the Assembly of the sixteenth century was concerned it never constituted any limitation upon the monarch's powers, for the simple reason that that chamber of loquacity never constituted an elective body, but was appointed by no other than the sovereign himself.[91] The origin of the autocratic state and the rise of the military landowning gentry Klyuchevsky masterfully explained mainly by two factors: continuous territorial expansion, and the urgent necessity of defending the frontiers of the wide-flung state. Precisely the same motives dictated the reforms of Peter I.[92] To the delight of the Slavophiles, Klyuchevsky exhibits these in the most unsparing colors. But he also has pages which would equally delight the Westerners: descriptions of the ruthless, shallow, dynastic struggles; the oppression and exploitation of the peasant in a truly Asiatic manner, with little concern for individual rights. The reason for the mutual satisfaction in both camps is that Klyuchevsky never wrote "patriotic" history though he was a Russian from tip to toe. He hated national glorification no less than national debasement. He felt with an equal sting of conscience the heart-rending ruthlessness of Ivan the Terrible and Peter the Great, the stupidity of boyar pettiness, the snobbery and class-selfishness of the later gentry, and the brutality and blind hatred of the peasants toward every form of social discipline.* But Klyuchevsky also understood the Russian character. He saw the causes lying behind the bloodstained pages of the past and therefore was able to draw from the story of the national past, not embittered and distorted ideas, but wholesome lessons. It would seem as if he always bore in mind the words of

---

* It is worth noticing that recently the Soviet state publishing house has turned once again to Klyuchevsky, and his *History of Russia* is being published after a lapse of nearly fifteen years.

Dostoyevsky: "Judge the Russian people not by the degrading sins which it often commits, but by the great and holy things to which, in the midst of its degradation, it constantly aspires.... Judge the people not by what it is, but by what it would like to become."[93]

Bestuzhev-Ryumin (1829-1897).—The list of nineteenth-century historians would be incomplete without the names of Bestuzhev-Ryumin and of one of his students, Platonov. Konstantine Nikolayevich Bestuzhev-Ryumin, pupil of Pogodin, Granovsky, and Solovyev, and great admirer of Karamzin, was among the first to steer an independent course in the stormy sea created by the Slavophiles and Westerners of the 'forties.[94] He was more of a critic than a historian, more of an eclectic idealist than an original thinker, an observer rather than a warrior, therefore a less colorful figure than his teachers; conservative, noncommittal, scholastically sterile, adhering to no particular school, he naturally had no historical Pléiade of his own and his disciples were not many; among them, the most distinguished was the late Platonov. Of noble birth and refined education, Bestuzhev-Ryumin came into academic life with impressive intellectual baggage, though, as he himself admitted, it was "chaotic," or, in the words of Pushkin, he had learned "something and somehow." His knowledge was not limited to history alone, but embraced also the fine arts, literature, theology, and philosophy; and he possessed no meager knowledge of the Russian chronicles.

As a professor of the University of St. Petersburg and a member of the Academy of Sciences, Bestuzhev-Ryumin always maintained that the historian must be impartial, giving nothing but the facts.[95] This principle he particularly applied to students, a device by which, as Platonov tells us, every pupil was considered an offshoot with its own root, which must not be hindered from growing. This impartiality led at times to incidents not much in his own favor and indicates how dangerous impartiality may become when applied without a sense of humor. Bestuzhev-Ryumin was a true product of the early Germanic school of Schlözer, in which authenticity and unbiased statement were placed before all else. Truly, before him "every bird lay unfeathered." Is it any wonder that Bestuzhev-Ryumin was overshadowed by such a giant as Solovyev and such an artist as Klyuchevsky? Today he is a half-forgotten man except as an object of curiosity for the student of Russian historiography. To him, however, the student must pay due tribute for his admirable collection of essays on a number of eighteenth- and nineteenth-century Russian historians and his scholarly analysis of the chronicles. His history of Russia (in two volumes), leading up to the death of Ivan IV, is an incomplete work which he had planned to extend through the nineteenth century. He also translated Henry T. Buckle's master work, the *History of Civilization in England*.

Platonov (1861–1933).—Among the "old guardsmen" and pupils of Bestuzhev-Ryumin, Sergey Feodorovich Platonov is preëminent.[96] Grandson of a serf and tutor of the royal heirs, a man of persistent energy and possessing also a religious reverence for his country's past, Platonov eventually gained recognition as a man of high scholarship. His main study,

The Nineteenth Century and Later 53

The Time of Troubles, is unique among its kind in its mastery of sources and presentation and in its sound conclusions. With genuine talent and Olympian patience, Platonov examined practically all the sources pertaining to this most complicated period in Russian history (1600-1613), selecting a few among the numerous biased presentations of chroniclers and other writers and narrating the notable developments in a most dispassionate way. Nothing escaped Platonov's vigilant eye, and the concatenated forces lying behind the whole social and political catastrophe, with all their consequences, are presented in masterly fashion. Particular attention has been given to the tense class struggle—between the old boyar class and the rising nobility created by Ivan IV, on the one side, and the urban and rural classes with their interlocking interests now coinciding, now in sharp conflict, on the other. The book received the highest praise of such scholars as Ikonnikov, Sergeyevich, and Klyuchevsky, and was recommended for the Uvarov prize.

Platonov, sane, well balanced, and reserved, was opposed to the materialistic interpretation of history.* It is not surprising that he found life uncomfortable during his last years. Yet he refused to leave his native land and loyally performed his duties as director of the library at the Academy of Sciences until he was forced to resign, shortly before his death, on the charge of concealing forbidden documents. He was exiled to Samara, where he died in great want in 1933.

---

*It is interesting to note that although Platonov has been violently condemned by Soviet historians, the Soviet state publishing house has recently issued a new edition of his capital study, *The Time of Troubles.*

Lyubavsky (1860-1937).—The heavy lot of Platonov during his later years fell also to his contemporary, Professor Matvey Kuzmich Lyubavsky. Lyubavsky belonged to the senior group of Klyuchevsky's pupils, though for his studies he chose a field somewhat remote from that of his colleagues; his interest was concentrated chiefly upon the past of Lithuania, a subject he selected for both his master's and his doctor's dissertations.[97] Those two bulky works immediately assured the writer an eminent place in his field. Written in a somewhat cryptic style and lavishly supported by references from firsthand sources, they represent a laborious task of investigation in the archives of western Russia. The caution with which the author elaborated his thesis, and the frequent citation of references rob it, however, of any literary charm. Like Bestuzhev-Ryumin, Lyubavsky left no school, but only a few individual students.

Lyubavsky's research led him to the theory that Lithuanian Russia, like Moscow, arose as a direct offspring of Kievan Russia. He elaborated this thesis in his lectures on early Russian history to the end of the sixteenth century, which he delivered at the University of Moscow. These may serve as a sort of supplement to Klyuchevsky's general course. If Presnyakov in his book, *The Formation of the Great Russian State,* felt that Lithuania had arisen as a consequence of political concentration, Lyubavsky, on the other hand, approached the same problem with an eye mainly to its ethnographic and geographic aspects, which led him to emphasize territorial concentration. While Lyubavsky saw in the union between the two principalities, Vladimir and Moscow, underlying military and financial causes, Presnyakov interpreted the same phenomenon as the outcome of a political tradition.

Very much as in his writings, Lyubavsky in person was detached from surrounding realities. In the full sense of the word he was an academician to whom politics and social activity were alien, his whole life being absorbed in his studies of the past, and his careful weaving of bygone events into a factual narrative. The Revolution was to him, therefore, a fatal blow; for a violent period demanded partisans and a colorful presentation of history, not a detached, objective narration of seemingly void events. His opponents sought Lyubavsky's removal from his post (he had been Rector of the University of Moscow), and they eventually succeeded. This event led to his banishment to Ufa, where he died a heartbroken man.

Presnyakov (1870-1929).—Along with Lyubavsky, of the University of Moscow, stood the figure of Alexander Evgenyevich Presnyakov, of the University of St. Petersburg. Presnyakov's doctoral dissertation, *The Formation of the Great Russian State,* displays an amazing knowledge of all the Russian chronicles and charters of the fifteenth and sixteenth centuries. The whole topic acquired a new significance and was presented in an entirely different light from that given by all previous writers.[98] Formerly, the rise of Moscow had mainly been interpreted not as the result of national and state aspirations, but as either the outcome of the greed of the landowning nobility (Chicherin), or—which was virtually the same idea (Solovyev, Klyuchevsky)—as the logical consequence of economic development leading to expansion.

Thus the Moscow prince was a mere tool either of individual landlords or economic circumstances, or both, and the state as such played only a subordinate part in national expansion. Presnyakov, throwing all these theories overboard, presented his own view, namely, that beneath all the strivings for territorial expansion was not mere individual greed, but a conscientious national aspiration and a political realization of the necessity of forming a consolidated state. The internal conflicts between Moscow and the other principalities, Tver, Suzdal, Ryazan, and others, were not simply expressions of the inherent pugnacious instinct of their respective princes, but rather expressions of conflicting ideas concerning the policy to be followed in the formation of a centralized national state. In other words, the whole internal conflict represented not the rivalry of acquisitive instincts, but a national centripetal force seeking the best methods for its materialization. The soundness of the theory may be questioned by some scholars, but the originality of the thesis is undeniable, as well as the fact that it stimulated the revision of many theories formerly held unchallenged.

Presnyakov's other works deal chiefly with recent Russian history. Among them must be mentioned his two short monographs on Alexander I and Nicholas I and his admirable short study of the Decembrist uprising. Under the influence of the Revolution, he inclined more to a popular writing of history, though even here he was careful to avoid waving the red flag. He died on September 30, 1929. The Society of Marxist Historians, of which he was a member, casually mentioned his death in their publication, *Istorik-Marksist* (of

The Nineteenth Century and Later

which, by the way, he was one of the editors), promising to give in the following issue a detailed appraisal of his works; but this promise has not been fulfilled.[99]

Lappo-Danilevsky (1863–1919).—Professor Alexander Sergeyevich Lappo-Danilevsky occupies a special place in Russian historiography, since he was never a historian in the narrow sense of the word.[100] He concentrated his ardent labor not upon Russian history as such, but upon history as a science in general. Whether his project happened to be of the broadest dimensions or only of a microscopic nature, it was invariably subordinated to his main subject, the methodology of history. Yet, here is something to be noted: in the voluminous works of Lappo-Danilevsky (which number 172 titles) the treatment of each individual topic, despite the fact that it is part of a larger scheme, constitutes a complete piece of work in itself, and each is, moreover, a masterpiece. His thesis on the system of taxation in the Muscovite state in the seventeenth century, for example, Milyukov has acknowledged to be "the most wonderful phenomenon in Russian historical literature." It is to be regretted that his writings lack the elasticity of style of a Klyuchevsky and the daring deductions of a Milyukov. This can be explained partly by the fact that Lappo-Danilevsky was a solitary person and very little in touch with the younger generation. He remained, instead, under the influence of the "juridical" school of Gradovsky and Chicherin long after it had been shelved by the advancing decades. Out of voluminous, hitherto unearthed sources he constructed a grandiose tower of antiquated design.

Lappo-Danilevsky focused his attention mainly upon the seventeenth and eighteenth centuries, to him an absorbing epoch, during which the crystallization of social and political Russia might be seen proceeding in most vivid fashion.[101] The emergence of a society with a new cultural physiognomy, new forms of economic life and judicial institutions, and a new sort of social consciousness, fascinated him. Distinguished contributions from his pen include monographs on the attachment of the peasants to the soil, the formations of various peasant classes, and a study concerning the *votchiny* (heritable estates) of the sixteenth and seventeenth centuries, which constituted the basis of the later structure of Russian society. His course of lectures on the eighteenth century at the University of St. Petersburg is interesting particularly in its organization. He divided the century into four parts: (1) predominance of the state; (2) decline of the state and rise of the nobility; (3) amalgamation of government and aristocratic interests, emancipation of the nobility, and early rise of public opinion; (4) severance of bonds between government and society and a period of reaction. Coincident with his enthusiastic research in this period, Lappo-Danilevsky also engaged in a work that would seem drudgery to others— the systematization of historical materials and their publication, including all the sources in foreign archives which concern Russia. He maintained that for an understanding of the relations between the Eastern Orthodox and the Western Catholic Church, as well as of Moscow's rôle in the Near Eastern problem, the Italian archives were indispensable. It was under his influence and instructions that the Academy of

The Nineteenth Century and Later 59

Sciences later sent its special correspondent to Rome. Simultaneously, he conducted an extensive investigation of all foreign residents in Moscow during the first half of the seventeenth century—their activities, the purpose of their journey thither, any service they might have given to the government or cultural influence they might have exerted. He wrote a notable essay on Peter the Great as founder of the Academy of Sciences; another on I. I. Betskoy and his system of education in the reign of Catherine II; and, incidentally, a third essay, on German-Russian relations in the eighteenth century. To Lappo-Danilevsky the final synthesis of history was to be the synthesis of mankind. But this goal was not to be attained merely by coining *a priori* formulae similar to those of Spencer, Comte, Hegel, or Marx, nor by intuitive, spontaneous thought; it was to be gained through an orderly, methodic understanding based on an intimate knowledge of the various stages through which humanity has passed in its long course which men call history.

Milyukov (1859-).—Among the few survivors of the "old guard," students of Solovyev and Klyuchevsky, is Pavel Nikolayevich Milyukov, ardent Westerner in the more modern sense, editor, lecturer, statesman, and author of a number of notable works on Russia.[102] His first work, which secured him a wide reputation as a historian, was his master's thesis, *State Economy in Russia During the First Quarter of the Eighteenth Century and the Reforms of Peter the Great*. This study embraced such a mass of new material extracted from the files of archives that it threw a flood of light upon many aspects other than the economic measures undertaken by

Peter I. It opened the way to other scholars, notably Professor M. M. Bogoslovsky, whose dissertation entitled *Local Reforms of Peter the Great* may be considered as a culmination of Milyukov's pioneering work. Later studies by Milyukov, such as his excellent essay entitled "Decay of Slavophilism," published in the periodical, *Voprosy, filosofii i psikhologii,* established him as an authority on Slavophilism, also, and his recent contribution to the study of Pushkin has demonstrated his impressive knowledge of Russian letters. Another work, *Main Currents in Russian Historical Thought,* is among the best studies in Russian historiography. It is unfortunate that the work was never completed; the first and only volume ends with Chaadayev and the influence of Schelling on Russian historical writing.

Milyukov's greatest work is his *Studies in the History of Russian Culture*. This is neither a chronological nor a "scientific" piece of work in an orthodox sense; yet it is valuable and refreshing because of its scope, its critical, realistic vision, and its uniqueness. It is an excellent supplement to Klyuchevsky's *Course in Russian History;* the two should be read together, since Milyukov filled in many of the gaps that Klyuchevsky left. Milyukov's first volume took up chiefly problems concerning population and national economic conditions. He showed most convincingly the total bankruptcy of the landed gentry because of its inability to adjust itself to the period following the reforms of 1861 and to the rising capitalistic form of production.[103] After discussing the underlying causes of Russian cultural backwardness, he concluded that the task of the future for Russia consists not in emphasis

The Nineteenth Century and Later 61

upon archeological remains of ancient times, which, it may be added, Milyukov considers as much overestimated, but in a common concentration of all efforts upon the building up of new cultural traditions in fruitful harmony with the social and political ideals of modern times.

The second volume deals with the church, sectarianism, and education, or, as the author says, the "spiritual" rather than the "material" aspects of culture. Here Milyukov reaches even more startling conclusions. An elaborate description is given of the breach between the masses and the handful of intelligentsia, first on religious grounds, later in other spheres. The urgent necessity of "catching up" with the west only widened the gap, since the vanguard of this force left the rear far behind. The chief cause for this lamentable state of affairs Milyukov seems to ascribe to orthodoxy, which had failed to become a powerful cultural lever, like the Protestant church in Europe and particularly in England. He neatly summarizes the situation by stating that in England religion nourished the citizen, and that culture there developed along with religious thought; hence the Englishman is still religious. In France the situation was different; religion took a definitely hostile attitude toward the development of modern scientific and philosophical thinking, and the national mind, advancing in spite of the church's resistance, left religion behind; consequently, the Frenchman turned against religion. In Russia, orthodoxy did neither one nor the other; it failed to keep pace with cultural development, and it did not establish an Inquisition; therefore the Russian intelligentsia became traditionally indifferent toward any religion.[104]

The third volume discusses "Nationalism and Public Opinion." A great deal of space is given to the archaic semi-Oriental political ideology of Old Muscovy, which was eventually forced to a clash with the incoming western ideas. The second part of this volume begins with the reforms of Peter, the rise of the modern intelligentsia, and its first encounters with the government. The conclusion one draws after a careful examination of Milyukov's thesis is that the future of Russia depends on the success of her adaptability to the course of Western civilization. The process, begun in the seventeenth century, will proceed in spite of the frequent opposition it is bound to meet, since it will be aided by the economic and political aggression of western Europe—a point of view particularly justified by the latest development in Soviet-German relations. Lately, Professor Milyukov has undertaken a revision of his *Studies,* and to date the first part of the first volume, and all of the second and third, have appeared. The political activities into which he plunged at the beginning of the twentieth century occupy much of his time. It is to be regretted that his energy has been so much diverted to other channels; Russia has few scholars like Milyukov, and his frequent absences from their ranks is keenly felt.

Semevsky (1848–1916).—The peasant question in Russian history has always been a vital problem around which have revolved many national issues. A good many Russian scholars have extended their studies of various phases of the peasant class beyond the confines of their own country. Writers like Chicherin, Belyayev, Dyakonov, Yanson, Myakotin, Lappo-Danilevsky, Bogoslovsky, Grekov, Kornilov, Khodsky, and

Mme. Efimenko have contributed much to the history of the Russian peasantry; Rostovtsev has enriched historical knowladge with his investigations concerning the Roman Empire; Vasilevsky and Uspensky have done the same for Byzantine history; Kareyev and Luchitsky have made sizable contributions to the study of the French peasants. However, almost all these studies have dealt with the earlier period of Russian history; few of the writers have gone beyond the eighteenth century, nor have they made any effort to embrace the vast field in its entirety. A task of this magnitude was undertaken and has been successfully carried out by Vasily Ivanovich Semevsky. This remarkable student and eminent authority on the history of the peasant, branded by his bigoted faculty colleagues as a "dangerous radical," and lately bespattered by pseudo-Marxian, epigonous writers who have labeled him the "petty bourgeois lacking a knowledge of Marxian dialectic,"[105] deserves a more objective presentation.

Whatever the contemporary opinion concerning Semevsky may be, his work will remain among the greatest contributions to the agrarian history of Russia, from which both friends and foes will draw material for many years to come. It is unfortunate indeed that his works are not available in other languages: historical literature might have been spared many mediocre and repetitious accounts of a subject that he so competently investigated long ago. His life illustrates the bitter cup that is put to the lips of the man who dares to go against the conventional views of his contemporaries.

Semevsky was born in the Province of Pskov, in the family of a poor squire; he was one of fourteen children and from childhood experienced want and struggle.[106] In 1866 he entered the St. Petersburg Medical Academy, where he spent two years and had the opportunty to study with the distinguished physiologist Syechenov and the world-famed Mechnikov. The two years contributed much to his character and immunized his mind to the various forms of intellectual sluggishness which years later afflicted the Russian intelligentsia. In 1868 Semevsky entered the University of St. Petersburg and devoted himself to the study of the history of, and social work among, peasants, whose economic problems became of absorbing interest to him for the rest of his life.[107] "It is high time," he wrote in 1881, "for our agrarian country, which has been maintained for a thousand years almost exclusively at the expense of the peasant, to pay due tribute to the class to which we owe everything."[108] Semevsky spent ten years on his master's thesis, which he presented in 1881, and revised and published in two volumes in 1903 under the title *Peasants in the Reign of Catherine II*.[109] For the first time there was revealed to the public a subject which until 1861 had been completely banned, and which after the lifting of the ban was still avoided by scholars because of its complexities. The warmest sympathy with the peasant did not hinder Semevsky from producing a work of singular merit, in which he demonstrated not only a stupendous knowledge of archival material, but also his especial talent for absorbing and properly interpreting sources.

The work was presented to the faculty, and here Semevsky first tasted the bitter fruit of reactionary criticism. Bestuzhev-Ryumin, to whom previous reference has been made, raised strong opposition to a subject which besmirched Russian history. It should be recalled that the year in which Semevsky was struggling for the acceptance of his dissertation was the year of the assassination of Alexander II. The presentation of his thesis was immediately followed by a reaction which sent a tremor among many panic-stricken faculty members. But the arguments of the guardian of "pure history" proved futile, since after all the study was a scholarly achievement, not a secondary account. Its author shifted the battlefield to Moscow, where his work was finally accepted. Among those who approved it was Klyuchevsky.[110] Upon the acceptance of his thesis and with his degree in hand, Semevsky returned to St. Petersburg to apply for a chair in Russian history, evidently with the intention of facing his opponents on an equal footing. To the surprise of all, he got the chair, though only for a brief period. Three years later, through the pressure of the same Bestuzhev-Ryumin,[111] he was forced out, despite the fact that he had become the most popular lecturer among the liberal students—and who was not a liberal student in those days? One of the main accusations made against him was that he presented Russian history in colors too black and dared to refer to so delicate a subject as the assassination of Paul.[112] Expulsion from the university was a terrible blow to his teaching career, and Semevsky, having always dreamed of teaching, was for a long time unable to become reconciled to giving it up. "Yes, my dear," he wrote some time later, "difficult and ungrateful is the work of the economist-historian."

There is no evil without compensating good. Deprived of his privilege of teaching, Semevsky was forced to concentrate his attention upon subjects that had claimed his early interest. His acquaintance with the work of Maurer was an incentive to him to make a similar study for his own country.[113] In 1888 there appeared his second capital work, *The Peasant Question in Russia in the Eighteenth and First Half of the Nineteenth Century,* a continuation of his previous study. The author was highly praised, was given the Uvarov prize, and was granted a gold medal by the Free Economic Society. In a short review an appraisal of this work is impossible: it is an exhaustive, classic study, not likely to be enlarged upon by future investigations. Every aspect of the problem—legal, political, social, and economic—is thoroughly analyzed. The author's conclusion is that emancipation of the peasants was made inevitable not by the will of the upper hierarchy in the capital, but by pressure of the masses in coöperation with the liberal intelligentsia; if in 1861 the reforms proved inadequate, as he later tried to show they did, it was because of unwillingness on the part of the government to carry the program to its logical end. It may be of interest to note that in this as well as in all his later works Semevsky expressed his approval of communal landownership, the abolition of which he thought would mean nothing less than economic ruin for the peasants.

For a long time Semevsky's attention was focused on Siberia, where he went in 1891 to study the labor situation in the gold-mining industry.[114] His wide travels and personal acquaintance with conditions, reënforced by use of the archives, enabled him to publish in 1898 a two-volume work entitled *Laborers in the Siberian Gold-mining Industry,* a study equaling in its thoroughness his previous works. In the following years he turned his attention to the liberal movement in Russia, and in 1909 published *Political and Social Ideas of the Decembrists*. For the first time the Decembrist movement was studied critically. The casual treatment of the subject by the court historians Bogdanovich and Shilder, by the "Westerner" Pypin, and even by the more conscientious Dovnar-Zapolsky was quite overshadowed by this book. Semevsky traced the rise of the Decembrist ideas from their earliest possible source in the eighteenth century to the increasing demand for liberal reforms which culminated in the first quarter of the nineteenth century in the Decembrist movement. He did not, however, deal with the organization of the secret societies nor with the uprising itself, but restricted his subject to the social and political origins of the movement.

Aside from these works, Semevsky contributed numerous articles to various magazines, most of which deserve wider publicity and point to the urgent advisability of collecting his entire works for publication at the earliest possible time. In 1913 he became editor of a well-known magazine, *Golos minuvshego* [*Voice of the Past*], an ambition he had dreamed of for many years; but death prevented his developing the editorial work as he had hoped. In an obituary notice a keen journalist neatly summarized Semevsky's career as follows: "Semevsky was barred from teaching in those sorrowful years when a similar fate befell M. M. Kovalevsky, S. A. Muromtsev, V. A. Goltsev, and even O. F. Miller, who was so little associated with politics. Militant liberals wanted to hold state positions and deliver lectures not held entirely reliable at an imperial hatchery of bureaucrats, and the ministers barred their path. What, then, was there for the balked champions to do? They took their accumulated learning which they could not deliver orally and transformed it into bulky volumes." These "bulky volumes" will prove a much more enduring monument to their authors than oral lectures delivered in crowded university auditoriums could ever be.

Shchapov (1830-1876).—Russian historical writing was predominantly Great Russian, and therefore bore a distinct "Moscow mark." Only a few men, very few indeed, endeavored to show that not all roads lead to Moscow. Among these are to be especially distinguished Shchapov, Kostomarov, Antonovich, Dragomanov, Hrushevsky, and others, who represented the "federal school," which rebelled against Great Russian particularism. One of the earliest to appreciate the significance of federalism in the political life of Russia was undoubtedly Afanasy Prokofyevich Shchapov, and if he failed to develop this thesis in his short lifetime, it was only because he was gagged by the bureaucracy.[115]

Shchapov was born in a Siberian village, Anga, about a hundred and fifty miles from Irkutsk. His father was Russian, his mother of Buryat origin. Very early he became interested in history and was a special admirer of Buckle; the recognized lights in Russian historiography did not quite satisfy him. The reason for this he explained in one of his addresses as follows:

> When I studied Ustryalov and Karamzin, it always seemed strange to me why in their histories one does not see rural Russia, a history of the masses, the so-called simple, dark people. Must

The Nineteenth Century and Later 69

the majority remain voiceless, passive, and inactive in history? Has not this overwhelming majority the right to enlightenment, to historical development, to life and importance, as have the nobility and clergy? ... Yet read the chronicles or the historical records up to the eighteenth century: who built, founded, populated, cleared the Russian soil of forests and drained it of marshes? Who, if not the peasant?[116]

In Shchapov's appeal can be discerned the earliest and the genuine *vox populi* in Russian historiography, a historical materialism, or, better still, a peasant materialism. With his characteristic wit, Plekhanov, in describing a debate between Shchapov and Chernyshevsky, referred to it as a verbal duel between a democrat and a social-democrat.[117] Like his much earlier predecessor, Ivan Pososhkov,[118] Shchapov was of the flesh and blood of the peasant, and the ideologist of his class. He approached the study of the past with the peasant's purely democratic interest, and history was to him a weapon for class defense, as well as a science.

For his master's dissertation, presented in 1858, Shchapov selected a subject which for political reasons students had not previously dared to attempt—the schism of the church in Russia. The new view taken in this thesis was contrary to all former views; the author concluded that the whole matter of the schism was a phenomenon not merely religious in nature but social as well. The merits of his study were acknowledged even by extremely conservative historians like Bestuzhev-Ryumin, who was usually very reserved in committing himself. From all indications, it is evident that Shchapov was one of the most brilliant writers of his time, but retarded in his intellectual growth by political circumstances.

While teaching at the University of Kazan, Shchapov became involved in a political affair for which he was exiled to Siberia. He had participated in a requiem mass for those who were killed in the peasant uprising at Bezdna in 1861 and had delivered a speech which ended with the sentence, "Long live a democratic constitution!"[119] In Siberia he gave his entire attention to the land of his birth, still considered by many Russians in the west as the icebox of the Empire to which only criminals were to be sent. Distressing material reverses and family troubles dimmed Shchapov's talent and shortened his life: yet he left behind him numerous articles, some constituting valuable contributions to the study of Russian religious sects, others giving a new and interesting view concerning federal tendencies in the history of Russia, particularly as demonstrated in the administration of Siberia.

If Shchapov, studying Siberia, came to be a firm believer in federal government as the only proper form for an empire the size of Russia, a number of writers drew similar deductions in studying the past of the Ukraine. Ukrainian historiography, for reasons that are self-evident, produced perhaps the largest number of "federalists." Among them stand out, first, the pioneer figures of V. B. Antonovich (1834–1908) and M. P. Dragomanov (1841–1895), both of whom were connected with the University of Kiev and were noted for their interest in Ukrainian ethnography and folklore.[120] Their compilation of the Ukrainian political folk songs accompanied by historical annotations was an excellent stimulus to the awakening of interest in a people considered secondary in importance, and in building up a school that was bound to produce po-

The Nineteenth Century and Later 71

litical repercussions. Small wonder that Dragomanov, who combined his historical research with journalism, found it uncomfortable at home and was soon forced to join the early political *émigrés* abroad—Herzen, Bakunin, and others. He became a lecturer at the University of Sofia, Bulgaria, and was the editor of the Bakunin and Kavelin letters. Antonovich wrote a number of monographs on the Ukrainian Cossacks, and edited a nine-volume collection of papers pertaining to southwestern Russia (*Arkhiv yugo-zapadnoy Rossii*).

Kostomarov (1817-1885).—A more colorful member of the Ukrainian "federal" school was Kostomarov. Nikolay Ivanovich Kostomarov was born in the Province of Voronezh. His father was a nobleman, who was killed by his own serfs; his mother was an Ukrainian, a former serf girl on his father's estate. It is probable that Kostomarov received from his mother both an interest in southern Russia and a sympathy for the peasants. He tells us of his reading and of the questions that arose in his mind, very much like those that Shchapov asked. "Why is it," he questioned himself, "that all histories talk about eminent statesmen, sometimes about laws and institutions, but disregard the life of the masses? The poor peasant, the tiller of the soil, seems not to exist in history. Why doesn't history say something about his general life, about the way he thinks and feels, about his happiness and his sorrows?" Kostomarov was evidently coming to a decision to accord to the peasant a place in historical literature.

In 1846 he joined the faculty of the University of Kiev, but a year later he was arrested as a member of the Democratic

Panslavist Cyril-Methodius Society, imprisoned for a year, and afterward exiled to Saratov. Not till 1859 was he allowed to renew his lectures in St. Petersburg. Kostomarov's interpretation of history was that later expressed by other historians of the national minorities, namely, that the historical process in Russia was of a centripetal nature, and that therefore more attention should be given to nationalities other than the Great Russian. Moreover, he insisted that the rôle of the state was being overemphasized when the masses were overlooked. This brought upon him the wrath of officialdom, the guns of the Slavophiles, and even the disfavor of the patriarch historian, Solovyev himself. Though Kostomarov enjoyed great popularity among his students, in 1862 he was forced to resign on the charge of political "unreliability."[121]

Kostomarov's chief works are concerned with the Ukrainian people and their struggle for independence against autocratic Moscow and aristocratic Catholic Poland. He emphasized ethnographic, rather than economic, history. In his works are many errors, chiefly a by-product of his varied activities, which allowed him insufficient time for thorough study—a fact that gave his opponents ground for labeling his work superficial.[122] A greater fault was Kostomarov's overenthusiastic interpretation of historical characters for whom he developed a personal fondness; he was apt to present them with a touch of dilettante romanticism. His chief contribution was not so much in his written works as in promoting an interest in Ukrainian history, which was almost totally disregarded by Great Russian writers since the Ukraine was generally thought of as being merely an annex to Moscow.

Hrushevsky (1866-1934).—The most notable figure among the "federalists" is unquestionably Hrushevsky. Mikhail Sergeyevich Hrushevsky studied at the University of Kiev, and later taught there for a brief period. Because of the inevitable difficulties into which his views would have led him, he moved to the University of Lwów (Lemberg), then in Austria, where he could enjoy greater cultural liberty. Here he became in a short time the leading figure among the faculty and built up a strong school. Hrushevsky was an eminent scholar and statesman; history to him was a weapon for defending his beliefs, yet he never failed to be first the scientific scholar. Unlike others, he never employed his historical knowledge for popular writing, propaganda pamphlets, or romantic narration, as did Kostomarov; his whole life was given to one cause: to erect for his people, in the form of a scholarly history, a monument which could neither be overlooked nor overthrown by his northern opponents.[123] His *History of Ukrainian Russia* is indeed a contribution to which Great Russian historians cannot remain indifferent. It is most unfortunate that the author, later distracted by the turbulent years of the revolutionary period, failed to complete this work, which he brought only to the middle of the seventeenth century. These nine bulky volumes are not a mere record of wars in which the Ukrainian people had to withstand the brunt of the onslaughts of both West and East, though these were many because their homeland was again and again the battleground of important historical conflicts; they contain, also, valuable accounts of the social, economic, and cultural history of Ukrainian Russia.

Hrushevsky's separatist tendencies compelled him to consider the Kievan period exclusively as Ukrainian history and not "Great Russian." Yet his thesis strongly suggests that, by treating each nationality—White Russian, Great Russian, and Ukrainian—in a fashion which justly ascribes due credit to each, Russian history generally will gain rather than lose, for only through such a treatment will the origins of Russia be fully appreciated, a better understanding be achieved, and unsound ideas be undermined. A realization of the continuous, successive development through the earlier periods that led up to the rise of Moscow will enrich our store of knowledge concerning both Great Russian and Ukrainian history. This development and these periods embraced Kievan Russia, Lithuania, and Poland, as well as Moscow, and the center should not be abruptly shifted from Kiev to the north without any proper explanation of the political and economic causes for this shift.

Hrushevsky was not a narrow historian. He felt acutely that a knowledge of political events alone will never be sufficient for an understanding of the past; hence his concentration on various aspects of the cultural life of the south. He was interested in philology, economics, sociology, and the natural sciences, and contributed countless articles in each field. His ceaseless political and literary activities, with all their adversities, hopes, and disappointments, finally shattered the sturdy champion, revered as the pride of his people. In 1934, after the loss of his sight, he died in the Caucasus, a total physical wreck. Hrushevsky left a contribution to historical literature which, regardless of political feuds, will always have to be taken into consideration if Russian history is to be seen in its entirety rather than as a series of episodic stages loosely revolving around the Muscovite state.

Siberian historiography.[124]—Closely related to the borderland provinces is the long-overlooked Siberian domain, which came to the attention of students in the eighteenth century when the future "father of Siberian history," Gerhard Friedrich Müller, was sent in 1733 as a member of the Kamchatka or "Great Northern" expedition to investigate the local archives. The fruit of Müller's ten years of labor in Siberia appeared in 1750 in a work entitled *A Description of the Siberian Kingdom,* and was followed in 1761 by additional chapters in his *Sammlung russischer Geschichte* [*Compilation of Russian History*],[125] which has been noted in our first view of this author's work. Though poorly constructed and dull in narration, the *Description,* together with a history plagiarized from it by Johann Fischer, quite adequately served its purpose by opening up a hitherto untouched field in Siberian colonization.[126]

For years thereafter, the subject of Siberia's past was handled mostly by amateurs like G. I. Spassky, who was by profession a mining engineer. His services, like those of other early amateurs, were mainly editorial. He was editor of two periodicals in which was published a large amount of source material, along with the accounts of travelers and newly discovered Siberian chronicles (the Stroganov and Esipov chronicles, and part of the Cherepanov). It was not until the middle of the nineteenth century that P. A. Slovtsov, in whom the local patriots saw the "Siberian Karamzin," took up the work of Müller in a more able manner, stressing somewhat the internal forces of colonization rather than the external, that is, those emanating from Moscow.[127]

In spite of certain errors, questionable methodology, and ponderous style, the merit of Slovtsov's work lies in the fact that for the first time the old idea of strictly chronological narration was abandoned. Even at that the author was very much handicapped, for to him Siberia was merely the "Russian back door to Asia and America" and therefore only an annex to the country at large—a view which explains why the whole past of that country has been recorded simply as a history of administrative measures. Furthermore, since the central government had as yet published very few of the papers kept in the capital, quite naturally Slovtsov was bound to defeat his own purpose. Whatever sources were available, he used; and he succeeded in composing two volumes, one covering the period of 1585–1742, a second the years 1742–1765. These volumes contain accounts concerning the conquest of Siberia, the character of the new administration, state trade, commerce, and industry, and the official policy toward the aborigines. In attempting to integrate this mass of information, however, Slovtsov demonstrated his inability to dissociate authentic from fictitious material, being apparently quite unaware that any such confusion existed.

The intensive publication of documents in western Russia by the Archeographical Commission and the Russian Geographical Society, the latter with branches in Siberia, stimulated further interest in the eastern province, while the growing local press and active publicists like N. M. Yadrintsev, and the appearance of Siberian Maecenases such as G. Yudin, I. Kuznetsov and I. Sibiryakov, aided considerably. The new type of student was best represented by Shchapov, of whom mention has previously been made. Here it may only be said that, among all his works, his essay on the ethnological development of the Siberian population remains to this day a significant contribution.

A second writer, a contemporary of Shchapov, to whom Siberian historiography is much indebted is S. S. Shashkov (Serafimovich) (1841-1882), whose essay on the ancient customs of Siberia (published in the *Otechestvenniye zapiski*, Nos. XX-XXII, 1867) gives an excellent account of the family status among the aborigines, of the church and clergy, the decaying morals, and the shameful exploitation of the natives by the administration and by individual entrepreneurs who sought quick fortunes. The essay brings to mind the remarkable similarity between the American Indian and the Siberian aborigine, whether with respect to economics, politics, or social conflict between native and invading stock.

For those who search for general chronological information, the compilation of data by I. V. Shcheglov will prove most useful.[128] Similar material about administrative measures and all sorts of statistical data will be found in the writings of Major General V. K. Andrievich, based mainly on the complete code of laws published by the government in the reign of Nicholas I.[129] A much more important methodological study was made by Professor P. N. Butsinsky (1853-1917), who in a series of monographs stressed above all else further archival investigation, without which he considered the writing of

Siberian history impossible.[130] Butsinsky's research on the settlement of Siberia was a significant landmark in the placing of Siberian historiography on a solid scholarly foundation. In it he lucidly elaborated the various methods by which Siberia was settled: by force of decrees, and by the action of exiled and voluntary settlers. Though the author failed by far to complete his original project, whatever appeared in print was based not only on published material but also on numerous manuscripts of the various archives of the Ministry of Justice and the Foreign Office. Unfortunately, the Siberian archives were barely looked at, a fact of which Butsinsky himself was well aware.

Other spadework was done by A. V. Oksenov, whose most noteworthy contribution was on the relations between Great Novgorod and Yugria and between Muscovy and Yugria. A. V. Adrianov compiled valuable data concerning Tomsk Province; P. M. Golovachev made a special investigation of the population of Siberia in the seventeenth and eighteenth centuries; and N. M. Yadrintsev, of the subsequent period.[131] Even more valuable service to Siberian historiography was performed by N. N. Ogloblin, who compiled a most thoroughgoing catalogue of the sources in the Siberian *Prikaz* (Bureau) as well as of many documents pertaining to Siberia in other Russian archives. What Ikonnikov did for Russian historiography in general, Ogloblin did for Siberia.[132] Equally important are the two works of V. I. Vaghin and S. M. Prutchenko on Speransky's administrative reforms in Siberia,[133] and I. P. Barsukov's two-volume work on the administration of Count Muravyev-Amursky.[134] Finally, there should be noted Tikhmenev's single study on the Russian-American Company, which constitutes part of the drama of eastern expansion that came to a climax in Russia's colonial establishments in America.[135]

A general survey of Siberian historiography in the nineteenth century plainly shows that a virgin soil was broken, but that little else was done. The first to attempt a general history of Siberia was Professor N. N. Firsov, in a course that he offered at the University of Kazan and at the Moscow Archeological Institute.[136] Though a secondary account, it represents an advance in the development of Siberian historiography, a transition from the merely compilatory to the synthetic.

Of the more recent writers, the foremost historians for Siberia are S. V. Bakhrushin and V. I. Ogorodnikov. The two complement each other: Bakhrushin's interest is concentrated chiefly on the general subject of colonization;[137] Ogorodnikov's study stresses the Siberian aborigines in relation to the incoming tide of Russian settlers and the development of the new administration.[138] Both authors endeavor to synthesize earlier historical writings. Economic and political developments in the Far East have led to a steadily increasing interest in Siberia, and the near future, it is hoped, will add much that is new to our knowledge of this long-neglected Russian domain.

Shakhmatov (1864-1920).—The study of Russian sources continued during the entire nineteenth century, culminating with the investigations of Aleksey Aleksandrovich Shakhmatov, a most remarkable linguist and one of the greatest authorities on the language of the chronicles. Shakhmatov's work is an example of the assistance that philology can offer the historian, especially the student of an earlier period.[139] His persistent analyses of the chronicles resulted in a series of revealing monographs and books, among which are the *Investigations Concerning the Earliest Chronicles, A Study of the Earliest Russian Language, A Study Concerning the Language of the Pskov Records,* and a number of others. These won high praise among Slavic scholars the world over.* Some of his views brought upon him severe criticism from the chauvinists of all the several camps. His conclusion that the Great Russian, Ukrainian, and White Russian languages, though originating in the Old Slavic, developed independently, stirred up sharp attacks by the extreme Ukrainians and White Russians, who denied any relationship with languages of Great Russia; equally vehement in their attacks were the Great Russians for his admission of any independent development, that is to say, his unwitting recognition of the existence of languages such as the Ukrainian and the White Russian.[140]

Shakhmatov's greatest contribution was in the field of chronology with respect to the chronicles. With amazing ingenuity and thorough scholarship he undertook to determine on a linguistic basis the approximate dates of the various sources, the Kievan, Novgorodian, and other chronicles. Thanks to his extraordinary linguistic equipment, Shakhmatov was able to disclose the interdependence of these

---

* Individual students like Alexander Brückner, Reinold Trautmann, or Samuel H. Cross are skeptical about Shakhmatov's deductions.

The Nineteenth Century and Later

sources, particularly in the matter of style. In his *Povest' vremennykh lyet* [*Annals of Ancient Times*], published by the Archeographical Commission in 1916, he accomplished what neither Tatishchev nor Schlözer, nor even Abbot Joseph Dobrovsky—who in 1812 first suggested the method later used by Shakhmatov—had succeeded in doing, because they lacked sufficient material for comparative study. This task was to discover "the most complete and most accurate, authentic" *Chronicle of Nestor*. Shakhmatov undertook the work not as a historian seeking facts, but as a philologist, and he achieved surprising results for his colleague-historians. By a masterful comparison of the chronicles, he not only conclusively established the dates of the various documents, but also the origin, place, and nature of the environment in which each document was produced, and the motives of the authors who wrote them. All this was a genuine revelation to many historians because it threw light upon several important moments in the course of Russian history, reclaiming, as it were, the outlook of contemporaries of these periods upon their own time as well as the past. Of course, many aspects remain obscure; some are based on sheer hypotheses, and Shakhmatov himself seems to accept them with much hesitation. Yet, notwithstanding these inevitable assumptions, Shakhmatov advanced the study of the chronicles to a point never dreamed of by historians of the eighteenth and even the nineteenth century.

Ikonnikov (1841-1923).—In the field of Russian historiography the name of Vladimir Stepanovich Ikonnikov is the most eminent. His four-volume work entitled *A Study of*

Russian Historiography stands not only as a unique achievement in scholarship, but also as a rare demonstration of phenomenal knowledge and of an amazing capacity to combine great quantity with a high degree of accuracy.[141] Of his other works, there must be mentioned his extensive monograph on Count N. S. Mordvinov, a study of the economic and political life of Russia in the early nineteenth century, and the annotated publication of documents pertaining to the peasant movement following the Decembrist uprising in 1825.

Pavlov-Silvansky (1869-1908).—In connection with the all-embracing national historical process outlined by earlier writers like Schlözer and Pogodin, and later by Klyuchevsky, Milyukov, and Hrushevsky, one name must not be overlooked—Nikolay Pavlovich Pavlov-Silvansky, who broadened the field in a somewhat different fashion. Pavlov-Silvansky destroyed the national shell in which many previous writers had enclosed feudal Russia. In his *Feudalism in Early Russia* and his later work, *Feudalism in Appanage Russia,* he introduced the logical theory that the entire Russian social structure, including serfdom, represented the same medieval structure of society as was familiar in western Europe. Premature death prevented this talented young student from further developing this thesis. All he had shown was the remarkable similarity between Russian and western feudalism in its legal aspects; social and economic aspects he had not touched.[142] But even within this limited scope Pavlov-Silvansky proved most undeniably the originality of his work and a masterful capacity for defending his views. He exploded all previous theories that the social structure of feudal Russia was peculiarly national with advantages that were unknown in the west. Lately, B. D. Grekov, member of the Russian Academy of Sciences, has taken up the work that Pavlov-Silvansky began, and his monographs promise further and more analytical study of a field in which much remains to be explored. The later Marxian writers wholeheartedly accepted Pavlov-Silvansky's theory, and extended it to economic and political aspects in general. Pavlov-Silvansky definitely proved, states Pokrovsky, that five hundred years ago Russia marched politically in step with western Europe, and what had to die in western Europe had also to die in eastern Europe; the only difference between the two was one of tempo.

Pokrovsky (1868-1932).—By the beginning of the twentieth century Russian historiography had prepared the ground not only for a thorough scientific approach to the national history, but also for a broader, more universal conception of that history. The works of Solovyev, Klyuchevsky, Milyukov, and Pavlov-Silvansky indicate an evolutionary progress which has reached its present stage with the rise of the Marxian School. This school has broadened the conception of Pavlov-Silvansky, in an endeavor to reinterpret the entire historical process in the light of universal economic developments by applying the methods of dialectic materialism. Georgy Valentinovich Plekhanov (1857-1918) began the Marxian reinterpretation, which he kept within the scope of cultural history. His *History of Russian Social Thought* represents one of the best of its kind. Unfortunately, the World War interrupted his work, which was carried only through the eighteenth century.[143]

Nikolay Aleksandrovich Rozhkov also endeavored to rewrite Russian history from a Marxist's point of view. But the cultural caliber of this writer was far inferior to that of Plekhanov; besides, his twelve volumes were written with such slovenly haste that the work failed dismally of its original purpose.[144] The only notable contribution of Rozhkov was his excellent monograph entitled *Agrarian Economy of Muscovite Russia in the Sixteenth Century*. Though even here the author in his usual haste committed many errors, these are not serious enough to undermine its general value, and the book has been quoted by many writers.

The father of the Marxian historical school in Russia was Mikhail Nikolayevich Pokrovsky. As a pupil of Klyuchevsky and Vinogradov at the University of Moscow, Pokrovsky received excellent training and very early proved himself not only a gifted historian but also one of those who vehemently refused to follow the beaten paths of their predecessors. In history he saw an effective political weapon, and with characteristic vigor he undertook the pioneering task of interpreting all Russian history from the Marxist's point of view, or, as he said, of transforming it from an "obscure literary form into a real, living, concrete fact." To him Marxism was a means, not a dogma, a powerful weapon, not an inflexible pattern, and history he used as a battleground on which to meet his political foes. Scarcely any other writer has worked out the Marxian conception so well as Pokrovsky has in his *Russian History;* nor has anyone ever equaled Pokrovsky's skill in subordinating history to politics. "History," he once said, "is politics fitted to the past." Whether or not one agrees

The Nineteenth Century and Later 85

with the author's presentation, one cannot deny his erudition and his talent. As a recent writer states, "No future student of Russian history will be able to dispense with his works or to find complete satisfaction in them."[145]

To Pokrovsky the Revolution was the hour of *a verbis ad verbera*. He had inherited from tsarist days a persecution complex, which later affords an explanation of his political conduct and his hatred of those who had once enjoyed a freedom of expression that had been denied to him.[146] A harsh critic, he spared no one, not even his colleagues, if they happened to be "class enemies." His acrid style made him a dangerous opponent: after the Revolution, many historians, some of them eminent figures such as Platonov, Lyubavsky, and Tarlé, suffered from the lash of his tongue, his piercing pen, and, most of all, his powerful political influence. Upon him rests a heavy moral responsibility for the utter routing of the older school and for the physical suffering inflicted upon its representatives, among whom were the most distinguished scholars of Russian historiography. His devastating criticism of Tarlé's interpretation of modern imperialism eventually resulted in Tarlé's imprisonment followed by exile to Central Asia.*

---

* See the list of imprisoned and exiled scholars in the *Slavonic Review*, April, 1933, pp. 711–713. The reader is also referred to an admirable account of the controversies that raged within the ranks of the Society of Marxist Historians and the sad lot that befell some of the men, by Stuart R. Tompkins, "Communist Historical Thought" (*ibid.*, January, 1935, 298 ff.). As an illustration of the vicious nagging of distinguished scholars by obscure stump-historians, the reader is referred to G. Zaidel and M. Tsvibak, *Klassovyi vrag na istoricheskom fronte. Tarlé i Platonov i ikh shkoly* [*The Class Enemy on the Historical Front. Tarlé and Platonov and Their Schools*] (Moscow-Leningrad, 1931).

After 1917 Pokrovsky gave much of his busy life to public affairs, sparing only "half an evening weekly" to historical research, as he states in his Preface to the second volume of his *History of Russian Culture*. As a leading member of the People's Commissariat of Education, he was responsible for doing away entirely with the teaching of history and replacing it by what was termed "social science." He was the editor of various collections of archival material pertaining to the Pugachev rebellion and to the Decembrist movement, and of the well-known periodical, *Krasny Arkhiv*. He was a founder of the militant Marxist Historical Society and of its publication, *Istorik-Marksist*, the aims of which were: (1) the maintenance of a united front of all Marxists engaged in historical research; (2) the study of Marxian methodology; (3) the combatting of all anti-Marxist and bourgeois distortions in historical writings; (4) the establishment of a Marxian critical literature; (5) assistance to its members in matters of research; and, finally, (6) the popularization of the Marxian historical view.[147] During his last years he was engaged in an elaborate publication of sources concerning Russian foreign policy since 1878.[148] He died in 1932, unaware that his school, so painstakingly established, was soon to fall under the axe of the very government that he had so loyally supported.

In recent years, changes have taken place in Russia in many directions, and not least in education and in the writing of history. After his death, Pokrovsky's star began to dim, at first slowly, but finally disappearing completely with the violent extinction of all the disciples of the father of Marxian historical writing. On May 16, 1934, the Council of People's

The Nineteenth Century and Later 87

Commissars and the Central Committee of the Communist Party passed a significant resolution in which it was frankly admitted that the teaching of history in the schools of the USSR was unsatisfactory. A survey of a number of schools as early as 1929 had revealed an appalling ignorance of history, a lamentably low intellectual level, and the absence of any original thinking by the pupils.[149] To remedy this situation the government issued in 1934 a decree which because of its importance I quote in full. It reads:[150]

DECREE OF THE COUNCIL OF PEOPLE'S COMMISSARS OF THE USSR AND THE CENTRAL COMMITTEE OF THE ALL-UNION COMMUNIST PARTY (BOLSHEVIKS)
[May 16, 1934]

CONCERNING THE TEACHING OF CIVIC HISTORY IN THE SCHOOLS OF THE USSR

The Council of People's Commissars and the Central Committee of the All-Union Communist Party (Bolsheviks) state that the teaching of history in the schools of the USSR is not administered satisfactorily. Textbooks and even the teaching are of an abstract, schematic nature. Instead of the teaching of civic history in a lively manner, the narrating of the most important events and facts in their chronological sequence accompanied by characterizations of historical figures, the students are given abstract definitions of social-economic structures, thus substituting for coherent narration of civic history, obscure schemes.

An essential requirement for the thorough mastery of history is the observance of a chronological sequence in the presentation of historical facts, personalities, and chronological dates. Only such a course in history can assure the student accessibility to, and clarity and concreteness in, historical records; on this basis alone can a correct analysis and synthesis of historical events be arrived at, which will guide the student to a Marxist understanding of history.

In accordance with this, the Council of People's Commissars of the USSR and the Central Committee of the All-Union Communist Party (Bolsheviks) decree:

1. By June, 1935, the following new textbooks shall be prepared: (a) a

history of the ancient world; (*b*) a history of the Middle Ages; (*c*) a modern history; (*d*) a history of the USSR; (*e*) a modern history of dependent and colonial countries.

2. Approval of the following list of members of groups entrusted with compiling the new historical textbooks shall be confirmed: [there follows the list of names.]

3. In order to train qualified specialists in history, the faculties of history at the Universities of Moscow and Leningrad shall be restored on September 1, 1934, with a contingent of students to be admitted in the autumn of one hundred and fifty for each of the faculties, the term of training to be five years.

Chairman of the Council of People's
Commissars of the USSR,

(Signed) V. MOLOTOV

Secretary of the Central Committee of
the All-Union Communist Party
(Bolsheviks),

(Signed) J. STALIN

The textbooks called for by the government were expected to stress sociological deductions and generalities less and facts more, to include descriptive biographies of historical personages, and to follow chronological order in telling the story of the past; historical writing was expected to be scholarly, and based on firsthand data—although what constituted scholarship or scientific method was not quite clear. A leading writer on the subject, A. Pankratova, defines them as follows: "To produce a scientific history textbook is to create a Bolshevik science. The problem in preparing a Bolshevik history textbook of any period is to demonstrate history in the light of our own grandiose epoch and the historical struggle of the laboring class for a proletarian dictatorship and socialism in the entire world."[151] From this elucidation it is quite evident that in present-day Russia political motiva-

The Nineteenth Century and Later 89

tion still remains a dominating factor in the writing of history. In this connection the scheme suggested by the officials for organizing the accumulated "scientific data" is interesting. As an illustration, Stalin has outlined the pattern for modern history as follows: (1) rise of modern capitalism, 1789-1871; (2) decay and defeat of capitalism, 1871-1918; (3) postwar imperialism and economic crisis: fascism and the struggle for colonies in western Europe; planned economy and triumphant socialist construction in the USSR.

The demand for a better knowledge of the ancient world was the first to be met. In July, 1937, appeared the first quarterly publication, entitled *Vyestnik drevney istorii* [*Messenger of Ancient History*], which includes the writings not only of Soviet historians but of recognized foreign authorities as well. Even here, Soviet patriotism leaves its imprint. "Since the history of the peoples of the USSR will always constitute an essential part of general history, we shall consider it our duty to study the problems of ancient history primarily as they relate to our motherland," announced one of the editors.[152] The new publication proclaimed that its main purpose would be a systematic study of the formerly oppressed peoples of the USSR, and for this purpose the editorial committee made an appeal to students of the Ukraine, White Russia, Uzbekistan, Kazakstan, Georgia, Armenia, Azerbeydzhan, and other parts of the Union to coöperate in the enterprise.

Simultaneously with the condemnation of the older textbooks and teaching methods, a revolt was in progress against the founder of the Marxist school, and he became a target of frequent attacks. It was pointed out that Pokrovsky began to write at the beginning of the twentieth century, at a time when "Marxism in Russia was quite widespread not only among the working class, but also among petty bourgeois and even bourgeois circles of the intelligentsia." It was also a time when opportunism flourished, giving rise to a school known as "Legal Marxists," condemned by Lenin himself. Pokrovsky, it was recalled, was closely associated with this heretical school.[153] Individual "artists in uniform" raised a chorus of protest against his historical method, and soon there followed a wholesale denunciation of the entire school that Pokrovsky had so painstakingly built up. Marxist writers suddenly threw overboard a ballast which only yesterday had been considered imperative for smooth sailing in Soviet waters; the impregnable truth of yesterday became the unforgivable error of today. The man who had been hailed as the "most devout and unswerving Communist, disciple of Lenin, consecrating all his powers to the struggle for the proletariat";[154] who had been proclaimed in dithyrambic terms the greatest historian and student of philosophy; who had rebelled against schematism in historical study; who had combatted "the vulgarization of dialectic materialism," and who had always been mindful of his Communist affiliations[155]—this man was now brought to a post-mortem trial and found guilty of the very heresies which he had formerly ascribed to his opponents. Pokrovsky is today accused of a too subjective conception of Marxism and is held responsible for its filtration into the writings of others; he is blamed for the arbitrary application of modern social and economic ideas to bygone generations that were utterly ignorant of them; he is criticized rather severely for his doctrine that Communism needed no objective science and for forcing the course of history into a Procrustean bed of materialism; finally, his rigid conception of Imperial Russia has come to be considered the worst historical blunder in his interpretation of the nation's past.[156] "He saw Tsarism as a static instrument of trade and capital, not as did Lenin, who saw in Tsarism, too, movement and development," and the Central Committee of the Communist Party specifically condemned the "vulgar, sociological views" of this former leader of the Marxian school, proclaiming that bourgeois subjectivism can only be defeated by a sufficient accumulation of objective knowledge.[157]

As the conflict between Stalinism and Trotskyism assumed Homeric proportions, the halcyon days of Pokrovsky's school faded completely away; it began to be associated with the heretical teachings of the opposition, and its members to be persecuted along with political opponents. Disciples of Pokrovsky were now proclaimed "enemies of the people, contemptible Trotskyst-Bukharinist agents of fascism," who were trying to smuggle anti-Marxist, anti-Leninist ideas of Pokrovsky into historical literature.[158] The new Soviet patriotism demanded a nationalistic interpretation of history, with a greater respect for the country's past. This tendency was aptly demonstrated by an incident in November, 1936, when the government suddenly suppressed the comic opera, *Bogatyri* [*Knights*], on the ground that the libretto, though written by the eminent Soviet poet, Demyan Byedniy, was not only historically incorrect, but was also "an insolent misrepresentation of the country's history." The official decree banning the luxuriously staged performance is illuminating, and the governmental exposition of its stand is worth quoting. It reads, in part, as follows:

It is well known that the Christianization of Russia was one of the principal factors in the *rapprochement* of the backward Russian people with the people of Byzantium and, later, with the people of the West; that is to say, with people of higher culture. It is also well known how important was the part that clergymen, particularly Greek clergymen, played in promoting literacy in the Russia of the Kiev period.

Marxists are not admirers of feudalism, and still less of capitalism. But Marx, Engels, Lenin, and Stalin many times noted in their works that at certain historical stages feudalism and, later, capitalism were instruments of progress in human history, promoting the productivity of labor and fostering culture and science. Thus, Byedniy's libretto reveals not only an anti-Marxist, but also a light-minded attitude toward history and a cheapening of the history of our people.[159]

The latest instructions to teachers of Russian history require that they explode the fascist theories of racial superiority and repudiate the humble rôle in the progress of humanity that has been assigned to the Slavs. The same document requires teachers to present the official adoption of Christianity in 988 by Vladimir as "an act of progress in the history of the Russian people"; the growth of Imperial Russia must be interpreted not alone as a result of the imperialistic gluttony of the Muscovite princes, but also as a natural, progressive, national development; the leaders in the struggle against Poland in 1612, Minin and Pozharsky, have now become true sons of the people, and the statement is supported by a reference to no other than N. Polevoy;[160] the war of 1812 against Napoleon must be shown as an act of elevated mass emotion—a united people rising against foreign occupation and in defense of national freedom. Finally, Peter I is to be introduced as a great statesman and a colorful historical figure.[161] No longer is he to be looked upon as a willful despot, but rather as a leader who conceived profound reforms and by his tireless activity awakened a dormant nation; a man whose conduct others must imitate in order to further western civilization and culture.[162] Not only have historical figures of the "Socialist Fatherland" undergone a total reinterpretation, but even historical dramas and operas have been changed to suit the recent demand for Soviet patriotism. Thus, Glinka's opera *A Life for the Tsar* has been revised and performed under the name of *Ivan Susanin*. Instead of the former chorus song,

> Glorify thyself, glorify thyself, Holy Russia!
> Upon the Russian throne ascends
> Our Russian legitimate Tsar!
> He comes to us in glory,
> Our Orthodox Sovereign-Tsar!

the modern version is:

> Glorify thyself, native soil.
> Glorify thyself, my native land.
> May forever and to eternity be strong
> Our beloved native land.

On August 22, 1937, the judges composing a special government commission announced the awarding of the second prize (75,000 rubles) for the most satisfactory textbook on the history of the USSR.[163] The first prize has not as yet been awarded. For the benefit of future writers the decision was accompanied by critical comments which constitute an illuminating document on the subject.[164] Omitting some of the more biased annotations, such as the one pertaining to the process of the Russian Revolution, the rôle played by the Communist Party, and the significance of the Stalin constitution, one finds others which point to a more constructive approach to historical writing, based, however, on a strictly national interpretation. The judges direct the attention of those who might in future strive for similar awards to blunders committed by previous students. The fact must be recognized, the warning states, that Christianity marked a step forward, and its introduction brought in certain elements of the higher Byzantine culture, and helped to spread literacy among the Slavs. Contestants must also not ignore the progressive rôle the monasteries played during the early days in Russia after Christianity had been officially adopted, when they were, indeed, valuable agencies in the promotion of literacy and colonial advancement. They must be able to discern in Bogdan Khmelnitsky's struggle against Poland and Turkey not mere violence only, but also a constructive national conflict for emancipation from foreign occupation. Similarly, the incorporation of the Ukraine and of Georgia into Russia shall be interpreted not solely as an act of imperialism, but as a result dictated by historical forces. Georgia, for instance, faced but two alternatives: either absorption by Persia and Turkey, or the protectorateship of Russia. Exactly the same sort of alternatives confronted the Ukraine, which was forced to choose between Poland and Turkey on one hand and Moscow on the other. Moscow was the more logical choice, since it seemed a lesser evil both to Georgia and to the Ukraine.[165] The jury also warned contestants against overidealizing earlier revolts, including such distinctly reactionary uprisings as those of the *Stryeltsy* [Moscow garrison] against the reforms of Peter I. Finally, one more criticism of particular interest, since it is clearly traceable to the latest foreign aggression against the Soviet Union, led chiefly by Hitlerite Germany. The judges direct attention to the fact that many of the contestants inadequately interpreted the significance of a number of past events, for example, the historical battle between the Novgorodians and Teutonic Knights on Lake Chudskoye (Peipus) in 1242. That battle, which ended in a fiasco for the Knights, marked the earliest defeat of the German plans for eastward colonization.

What are the immediate prospects for Russian historiography so far as the Soviet Union is concerned? The expulsion of Trotskyism brought also a "purge" of the historians. A vicious campaign was begun against numerous prominent Soviet historians: writers like Piontkovsky, Vanag, Friedland, Oksman, M. Lurye, and others were suddenly discovered to be "agents of Trotsky," or "smugglers" of the no longer fashionable ideas of Pokrovsky.* From all indications, it seems

---

* *Pravda*, May 11, 1937. Strangely enough, Trotsky himself does not accept Pokrovsky as a master of Marxism. "While taking due cognizance of the erudition, conscientiousness and talent of the deceased scholar," he writes, "it is impermissible not to state that Pokrovsky failed to master the method of Marxism, and instead of providing an analysis of the continued interaction of all the elements in the historical process, he provided for each occasion mechanistic constructions *ad hoc,* without bothering about their dialectic interconnection."—L. Trotsky, *The Stalin School of Falsification* (New York, 1937), xxx–xxxi.

clear that the hunt has only begun. Unquestionably, historical writing in the Soviet Union today is facing one of its gravest crises: the sudden readjustment from "universal materialism" to an indigenous nationalism has left many students in the "lampless depths of historical mystery." No one dares to write, for no one can tell what interpretation will be next announced. Crucial questions in Marxian historiography—the rôle of the individual in history, the relations between economic and social factors, or what constitutes scientific history—remain unanswered. Soviet historiography is at the crossroads, and, alas, whichever way it goes, serious political interference with scholarship probably lies in wait.[166]

A convenient illustration of historical interpretation to satisfy the official taste is that of Tarlé. In 1937 Professor Eugene Tarlé in his book, *Bonaparte*,* wrote:

Never did Napoleon, or his marshals, or their companions in arms, speak of the war of 1812 as a "national" war, in the same sense that they spoke of the Spanish guerrilla war as a "national" war. Nor could they compare the two phenomena. The war in Russia lasted six months. Of these six months, the first three saw Napoleon constantly victorious as he advanced along a direct line from Kovno to Vilna to Smolensk to Moscow, interrupted by battles and petty skirmishes with the regular Russian army. There was, however, not a single national mass revolt against the French—neither then nor after Napoleon's entry into Moscow. Indeed, there were occurrences of quite a contrary nature, as when the peasants of Smolensk complained to the French authorities that their master, the landowner, Engelhardt, had been guilty of betraying the French.... The peasants as a group took no part in these activities.... It is clear that if the Spanish guerrilla war-

---

* New York, Knight Publications, 1937, 302–303.

The Nineteenth Century and Later

fare might justifiably be called a national war, it would be impossible to apply this term to any Russian movement in the war of 1812. People began to regard even the burning of Smolensk and Moscow and the firing of villages as manifestations of "national war," overlooking the fact that these were systematic acts of the Russian army in its retreat to Moscow.

For this interpretation Professor Tarlé was seriously reprimanded. Only a year later, in his new book, to appease the wrath of the lords of the state, the author wrote* in his new book, *Napoleon's Invasion of Russia:*

The guerrilla movement that began immediately after the battle of Borodino, as we shall see further, could have attained success only by means of the most active voluntary aid sedulously rendered by the Russian peasantry. This insatiable hatred toward the usurpers, marauders, and oppressors, ignorant of whence they came, was expressed by the way in which the Russian peasants joined the army in 1812 and how they fought. The national character of this war could express itself immediately in the organized form—the army.... Further, in describing the retreat of the Grand Army, I refer in detail to the guerrilla warfare, to the participation in it of the peasants.... According to the unanimous opinion of the French, absolutely nowhere except in Spain did the peasants in the villages show such desperate resistance as in Russia. "Each village was transformed at our approach into either a bonfire or a fortress":—so the French wrote afterwards.... It was precisely the peasant who destroyed the magnificent cavalry of Murat, first in the world, under whose victorious onslaught ran all European armies; it was this very army that the Russian peasant destroyed.... One cannot write in the history of 1812 a separate chapter on "The National War." The *entire* war against

---

* *Nashestviye Napoleona na Rossiyu. 1812 god.* [*The Invasion of Russia by Napoleon, 1812*], 182–184. This book is soon to be published by the Oxford University Press.

the invading Napoleon was solidly a national war. Napoleon counted in his strategy the number of his troops and the troops of Alexander, but he had to fight with the Russian people, whom Napoleon had forgotten. It was the people's arm that inflicted upon the greatest commander in world's history the irreparable, fatal blow.

Emigré historians.—Something must be said, if very briefly, about those students of Russian history who through political circumstances find themselves on foreign soil. The lives of the majority of these men are by no means enviable: material want, lack of library facilities, the necessity for cultural readjustment, sometimes a callous environment poisoned with bigoted nationalism—all this is not conducive to the inspiration of the Russian scholar abroad. And still, despite the cold foreign wind that has threatened to extinguish the flickering lamp of scholarship, it has been kept burning at the price of enormous hardships ever since the year of the exodus, 1921. It is estimated that more than nine hundred works in about ten different languages have been produced in the last seventeen years, including books, monographs, and articles. The articles, for obvious reasons, are the predominant form of writing, since they involve the least financial outlay.[167] Though handicapped by distance and by political feuds, some *émigrés* have succeeded in organizing historical societies, among which are mainly to be noted the Kondakov Institute and the Russian Historical Society, both of them in Czechoslovakia, and the Russian Archeological Society, in Yugoslavia. Needless to say, the existence of these associations is precarious. Herculean efforts must often be exerted to keep them intellectually alive, and the general political confusion on the

Continent promises no bright future for these cultural islands in stormy alien seas, as the fate of Czechoslovakia has recently shown.

The subjects of study undertaken by the *émigré* historians vary widely. Men who have found shelter in the Slavic countries seem to concentrate upon early Russian history; among these are A. L. Pogodin, A. V. Florovsky, and L. G. Bagrov; M. V. Shakhmatov and E. Y. Perfetsky are engaged in a revaluation of the chronicles; I. I. Lappo has published his capital work on the Lithuanian statute of 1588; M. I. Rostovtsev has published his well-known monographs on southern Russian archeology;[168] D. N. Odinets and V. A. Myakotin took up respectively the annexation and the social history of the Ukraine; P. B. Struve will soon publish an economic and social history of Russia; S. G. Svatikov has made a pioneering investigation of the Don Cossacks and their relations with Moscow, and another in the history of Siberian administration in the nineteenth century; M. M. Karpovich is preparing a manuscript on the revolutionary movement of Russia; G. V. Vernadsky has published a thorough account of Novosiltsov's constitutional project of 1820[169] and is now engaged on an ambitious scheme of rewriting Russian history according to the views of the Eurasian school—a school which deserves attention even in an outline of Russian historiography.

The Eurasian school.—The Eurasian school emerged amidst the political chaos of the *émigré* life of the Russian intelligentsia in Yugoslavia in 1921. The school embraces various outlooks upon national life—political, social, economic, religious, philosophical, and historical. I shall limit my discussion exclusively to the historical outlook.* The conception of history held by the Eurasians is somewhat as follows. Former writers seem to have accepted the national growth of the Russian Empire as an organic, uninterrupted, single process, modified of course in some measure by influences coming from east and west. But influences were considered but casual factors and regardless of them Russia would have flourished in all her imperial glory; they never deeply penetrated the national core; they left few visible marks on the national character or the political body. Prior to 1917 the courses in history were usually divided into Russian and Western history, two entirely separate subjects; the western border of the Empire was a sort of Chinese wall separating two different worlds. The Westerners of the nineteenth century were the first to raise their voices in favor of Russia's inseparable bond with western Europe, though that "bond" has hardly ever been clearly formulated. They referred to the Russian people as a European nation which had passed through stages of development similar to those of nations on the Continent; yet on Russia's part the dividing line remained—"We and the West." The situation was not much different with respect to the opposite, eastern border of the Empire. If the west represented to Russians a world by itself, a living body, the eastern borderland, on the other hand, was considered by Russian historians as simply a void space, a "geographical expression" that was little heeded except by orientalists like Bartold.[170] Former

* The mouthpiece of the Eurasian philosophy is Prince N. S. Trubetskoy, whose earliest work, *Evropa i Chelovechestvo* [*Europe and Mankind*] (Sofia, 1920), was the forewarning flash on the *émigré* intellectual horizon.

writers, including Solovyev, Klyuchevsky, and Milyukov in the earlier editions of his *Studies in the History of Russian Culture,* when they referred to the geographic foundations of the Russian state had in mind chiefly the so-called "European" or "west of the Ural Mountains" Russia. The dominance of the Mongols was scarcely mentioned, not even by Klyuchevsky in his monumental five-volume history, and others referred to the Mongolian invasion as a mere episode, a raid of ferocious hordes who descended from Asia and, like a cancer, began to consume the vitality of the state. This plague lasted for a certain number of decades; then came a realization of the situation, which led suddenly to the expulsion of the despicable Mongols, and Russia was once again freed from foreign intruders.

Just as American scholars now endeavor to correct the outlived provincial concept of United States history in the light of what they call Euro-American development, so the Eurasian school is making an effort to reinterpret Russia in a Euro-Asian light.* It attempts to correct the manifest error of interpreting the eastern border as a void space by showing it to be a present factor in the life of the nation, and is thus presenting a new concept of the Russian historical process. The very essence of this process, it maintains, is the fact that the former Empire—the present USSR—constitutes, in itself, a historic-geographic world. Such an interpretation coincides with that of individual students, for example, P. N. Savitsky,

---

* I take this opportunity to thank Professor Herbert E. Bolton, of the University of California, for reading to me separate chapters from his forthcoming book entitled *The Western Hemisphere: Its Historical Development,* in which he develops the Euro-American idea.

who presents a similar conception with emphasis upon its geographic aspect.[171] Though Moscow began to colonize the territories beyond the Urals only at the end of the sixteenth century, even from the earliest times the fate of the Russian tribes has been closely knit with that of the other peoples of Eurasia: for in those very early centuries they came in contact with the Iranian, Finnish, and Turco-Mongolian tribes, and thus was formed, through this interrelationship, the backbone of the later vast Empire.

In his book *Nachertaniye russkoy istorii* [*An Outline of Russian History*] and his more recent study *Zvenya russkoy kultury* [*Links in Russian Culture*],[172] Professor Vernadsky, of Yale, a member of the Eurasian school, has brought to the attention of the general reader the following interrelated facts: that Asia is as much a part of Russia as the west is, if not more so; that central Asia played an extremely significant rôle in the past of the people, a fact never to be overlooked; that from the earliest days and until the time when Moscow established her autocratic form of government, the people of the southwestern plains and of the north were in continuous communication with the eastern tribes; and, lastly, that the Gargantuan territorial appetite of Genghis Khan gave rise to the imperial designs of the tsars, and that these have lately become also the policy of the USSR. All these things really represent a series of traditional acts in a single historical drama.[173] Both the century-long westward expansion of the Mongols and the later eastward expansion of the Russians, Vernadsky maintains, were dictated by "geopolitical" conditions and a common striving for the realization of one and

The Nineteenth Century and Later 103

the same idea—a Eurasian state.[174] Convincing as this theory may now seem, it lay dormant until the Eurasian school made it the alpha and omega of Russian history, and to men like Vernadsky and Savitsky[175] belongs the honor due to pioneers. They came out as advocates of a new presentation of the dreaded Mongolians—formerly the symbol of destruction, or of a negligible occurrence or a temporary elemental force, but now to be considered a mighty, constructive factor in molding Imperial Russia.

When the Eurasian school refers to the "Russian people," it has in mind not only the Great Russians, but also the Ukrainians and White Russians, each of whom represents a cultural branch of the Eastern Slavs, though politically they stand together. Moreover, in the history of Eurasia these peoples occupy only a segment of an entire "geopolitical unit." The merit of such a conception is that it compels the threefold study—social, economic, and cultural—of all parts of this "sixth of the world," rather than a study of the political center alone; a view which coincides with that of Dragomanov, Antonovich, Shchapov, and other students of the above-mentioned "federal school." Furthermore, by acknowledging cultural debts in both eastern and western directions, the Eurasians believe, historical science will advance far beyond that of their predecessors, the Westerners and the Slavophiles.

To conclude, Vernadsky and Savitsky maintain that, in the future, Russia must be considered a "geopolitical unit" on a Euro-Asiatic scale, and that its past must be presented not only in a chronological but also in a "spatial" form. Geography therefore must play a significant part, and the growth of the nation must be traced parallel with the geographic factors involved; hence, Vernadsky's coined term, "myestorazvitiye," best rendered into English as "place-development," now generally accepted even by his strong opponent, Milyukov.[176] Here, however, the Eurasian school reveals its Achillean heel: the "geopolitical" aspect of the historical development of Russia—the "Eurasian idiographic singleness"—is still obscure and needs further and clearer exposition; otherwise, it will be doomed to remain what one biting critic of the Eurasians has called "geopolitical mysticism." Nor has this school succeeded in explaining with sufficient clarity the underlying forces in the political make-up of Eurasia: psychological similarity alone is hardly enough to bring one-sixth of the earth under a single flag. Other forces as well, the economic, for example, have driven this immense number of peoples into a political family. Finally, the overemphasis upon the uniqueness of Eurasian civilization and on special qualities of the "Turanian" peoples leads one to fear that earlier blunders of the Slavophiles of blessed memory may be repeated.[177] Yet, despite certain shortcomings and sharp criticism from almost every political camp, it must be remembered that the Eurasian school is pioneering, groping toward distant horizons, and only beginning to gain respectful recognition; it has already opened up to history a newer and broader view, which the future student will be unable to disregard. A fertile ground has been broken by these men, a new seed sown, and a rich harvest is certain to follow.[178]

Conclusion

In reviewing the accomplishments of Russian historiography in the last hundred and fifty years, what are the most notable features, and what are the immediate prospects for the future? It is indisputable that the nineteenth century and the prerevolutionary period of the twentieth century showed amazing progress both in the publication of sources and in the writing of history. With the direct encouragement of the government and of private individuals, special societies have been formed which have commenced publishing activities on a gigantic scale. The most notable of these organizations is the Archeographical Commission, which has already published a staggering amount of source material. Simultaneously with this feverish activity there has progressed the art of paleography and the study of chronicles, culminating with the latest investigations by Shakhmatov. Equally impressive results have been achieved in the study of special periods by men like Platonov, Lyubavsky, and Presnyakov. In the field of monographic subjects, legal and agrarian history, and the Petrine epoch, a number of students have been no less distinguished: suffice it to recall the names of Sergeyevich, Semevsky, and Bogoslovsky. In the realm of "federal" history may be recalled the names of Shchapov, Kostomarov, and Hrushevsky; and finally, in the work of synthesizing the past twelve centuries, solid foundations have been laid by Klyuchevsky, Milyukov, and Pokrovsky, divergent, indeed, in views, scope, and method of approach, yet suggestive, stimulating, and capping the efforts of many preceding generations.

Nevertheless, as time goes on one cannot escape the realization that the legacy of Russian historiography opens avenues for wider interpretations, and that freshly unearthed sources, steadily growing in amount, require analysis in the light of recent events, and that a "revaluation of many old values" is becoming most desirable. The Revolution has temporarily allowed the stump speaker to dominate historical writing. But as years go by, the pendulum will swing back, indicating the restoration, if not yet of a completely objective, at least of a saner, approach to the past. A number of conditions, both internal and external to the country, make it imperative to restore, overhaul, and eventually revise the rich past of the nation. Many topics urgently await the historians of the newer types; for example, the growth-process of the Russian Empire, the rôle of the border states (*okrainy*), the ideas of federalism prevailing in the Empire, the Eurasian interpretation, the foreign and colonial policies of the Imperial government, particularly eastward (Siberian history is still mostly an unexplored field), the biographical reinterpretation of historical figures. As for the history of the present turbulent time, it is definitely a subject for writers of the future. Attempts to write the history of the Russian Revolution have proved unsuccessful even for mature scholars of the caliber of Milyukov or Pokrovsky, who sadly failed in their endeavor to give a historical account of this latest Russian drama. The entire significant epoch is still too near to admit of proper appreciation or of being seen in its due proportions. Practically everything written on the Revolution is so strongly biased that it will be of little value to the future historian except as it may serve to display the opinions of contemporaries in the various political camps, or of mere onlookers who could not withstand the temptation to narrate their dramatic experiences. In this respect we who are contemporary observers can aid the future historian in his task of interpreting our own era by assuming the more humble rôle of the *Geschichtssammler*. Thus, in one field at least, we, too, begin at the same point at which the historian of the eighteenth century started.

NOTES

[1] N. A. Popov, "Ucheniye i literaturniye trudy V. N. Tatishcheva [Scholarly and Literary Works of V. N. Tatishchev]," *Zhurnal ministerstva narodnogo prosvyeshchevniya,* June, 1886; idem, *Tatishchev i ego vremya* [*Tatishchev and His Times*] (Moscow, 1861).

[2] A. N. Pypin, *Istoriya russkoy literatury* [*History of Russian Literature*] (St. Petersburg, 1911), III, 369-370.

[3] *Russky biograficheshy slovar* [*Russian Biographical Dictionary*], XX, 342-343.

[4] P. P. Pekarsky, *Noviye izvestiya o V. N. Tatishcheve* [*New Information Concerning V. N. Tatishchev*] (St. Petersburg, 1864).

[5] V. N. Tatishchev, *Istoriya rossiyskaya s samykh drevneyshikh vremyen* [*Russian History from the Earliest Times*] (5 vols.; Moscow, 1768-1848. The five volumes were published posthumously).

[6] Pypin, *op. cit.*, III, 372.

[7] *Sbornik II otd. russkogo yazyka i slovesnosti Imperatorskoy Akademii Nauk,* XXX (1883), 51-53; Popov, *Tatishchev i ego vremya* [*Tatishchev and His Times*], 591-598.

[8] K. N. Bestuzhev-Ryumin, *Biografii i kharakteristiki* [*Biographical Essays*] (St. Petersburg, 1882), 141, 145-146, 147.

[9] G. F. Müller, *Opisaniye Sibirskogo tsarstva* [*A Description of the Siberian Kingdom*] (St. Petersburg, 1750); *Sammlung russischer Geschichte* (9 vols.; St. Petersburg, 1732-1764. A posthumous volume, the tenth, was published in 1816 in Dorpat).

[10] G. S. Bayer, *De Varagis* (St. Petersburg, 1768); *De origine et priscis sedibus Scytharum* (St. Petersburg, 1728); *Auszug der älteren Staatsgeschichte* (St. Petersburg, 1728).

[11] P. P. Pekarsky, *Istoriya akademii nauk* [*History of the Academy of Sciences*], I, 381.

[12] N. N. Golitsyn, *Portfeli G. F. Millera* [*The Portfolios of G. F. Müller*] (Moscow, 1899).

[13] *Akty istoricheskiye, sobranniye i izdanniye arkheograficheskoyu kommissieyu* [*Historical Documents, Collected and Published by the Archeographical Commission*] (5 vols.; St. Petersburg, 1841-1842); *Dopolneniya* [*Supplements*] (12 vols.; 1846-1872).

[14] P. P. Pekarsky, *op. cit.*, I, 418-424.

[15] A. L. von Schlözer, *Allgemeine nordische Geschichte* (Halle, 1771); *Verstellung seiner universal-historie* (Göttingen, 1772); *Histoire universelle* (Tübingen, 1781); *Neuverändertes Russland, oder Leben Catharina der Zweyten* (Riga, 1771–1772); *Probe russischer Annalen* (Bremen, 1768); *Nestor: russische Annalen in ihrer slavonischen Ursprache verglichen, gereinigt und erklärt* (Göttingen, 1802–1809).

[16] *Sbornik II otd. russkogo yazyka i slovesnosti Imperatorskoy Akademii Nauk*, XXX (1883), 1–3, 25, 30, 44.

[17] Pekarsky, *op. cit.*, I, 378.

[18] Bestuzhev-Ryumin, *op. cit.*, 201–202.

[19] *Russky biograficheskiy slovar*, XXIII, 343–344.

[20] M. O. Koyalovich, *Istoriya russkogo samosoznaniya* [*History of Russian Self-realization*] (St. Petersburg, 1893), 110–111.

[21] A. N. Pypin, *Istoriya russkoy etnografii* [*History of Russian Ethnography*] (St. Petersburg, 1890–1892), I, 19–20.

[22] V. Myakotin, *Iz istorii russkogo obshchestva* [*Notes on the History of Russian Society*] (St. Petersburg, 1902), 112 ff.

[23] M. M. Shcherbatov, *Neizdanniye sochineniya* [*Unpublished Works*] (Moscow, 1935), 112–113; *Russky biograficheskiy slovar*, XXIV, 115.

[24] M. M. Shcherbatov, *Istoriya rossiyskaya ot drevneyshikh vremyen* [*Russian History from the Earliest Times*] (7 vols.; St. Petersburg, 1774–1805. German translation, Danzig, 1779).

[25] Nicolas Gabriel Le Clerc, *Histoire de la Russie ancienne et moderne* (Paris, 1783–1794).

[26] I. N. Boltin, *Kriticheskiye primechaniya gen.-mayora Boltina na pervyvtoroy tom istorii knyazya Shcherbatova* [*Critical Notes of Maj. Gen. Boltin to Volumes I and II of the History of Prince Shcherbatov*] (2 vols.; St. Petersburg, 1793–1794); *Otvyet gen.-mayora Boltina na pismo Kn. Shcherbatova* [*Reply of Maj. Gen. Boltin to a Letter of Prince Shcherbatov*] (St. Petersburg, 1793); *Primechaniya na istoriyu Rossii gospodina Leklerka* [*Critical Notes to the History of Russia by M. Le Clerc*] (2 vols.; St. Petersburg, 1788).

[27] *Russky biograficheskiy slovar*, III, 199–200.

[28] *Ibid.*, III, 193–194.

[29] Pypin, *Istoriya russkoy etnografiii*, I, 147 ff.

[30] Nestor, annalist (d. 1115?). See *La Chronique de Nestor*, tr. en français d'après l'édition impériale de Pétersbourg, manuscrit de Königsberg (2 vols.; Paris, 1834–1835). Another translation is by L. Leger (Paris, 1884). There is a translation of Schlözer's *Nestor* in Russian by Yazykov. See also

the later edition, *Die altrussische Nestorchronik, Povest vremennykh lyet* [*Annals of Ancient Times*], tr. by R. Trautmann (Leipzig, 1931).

[31] Pypin, *Istoriya russkoy literatury*, III, 510; *Sbornik II otd. russkogo yazyka i slovesnosti Imperatorskoy Akademii Nauk*, XXX (1883), 193-195.

[32] V. S. Ikonnikov, *Opyt russkoy istoriografii* [*A Study of Russian Historiography*] (2 vols.; Kiev, 1891), I, Bk. 1, 297-299.

[33] Ikonnikov, *op. cit.*, I, 135 ff. A graphic account concerning Rumyantsev's rôle in collecting national sources may be found in *Sobraniye gosudarstvennykh gramot i dogovorov* [*Collection of State Charters and Treaties*], V, ii–xiii. For a more detailed study, see A. A. Kochubinsky, *Admiral Shishkov i Kantsler gr. Rumyantsev. Nachalniye gody slavyanovedeniya* [*Admiral Shishkov and Chancellor Rumyantsev. Initial Years of Slavic Studies*] (Odessa, 1887–1888); *Vyestnik Evropy*, X (1888), 703 ff.

[34] *Sobraniye gosudarstvennykh gramot i dogovorov* [*Collection of State Charters and Treaties*] (4 vols.; Moscow, 1813–1828. A fifth volume appeared in 1894).

[35] Ikonnikov, *op. cit.*, I, Bk. 1, 150.

[36] *Ibid.*, 149–150.

[37] *Ibid.*, 164.

[38] The nature of these sources is discussed by A. Starchevsky in *Zhurnal ministerstva narodnogo prosvyeshcheniya*, XLIX (1846), 14–40.

[39] A. A. Kochubinsky, *op. cit.*, 70–75; also Appendix, vii ff.

[40] A. Starchevsky, "O zaslugakh Rumyantseva, okazannykh otechestvennoy istorii [The Services of Rumyantsev to Native History]," *Zhurnal ministerstva narodnogo prosvyeshcheniya*, XLIX (1846), 1 ff., 51–56; Kochubinsky, *op. cit.*, pt. 2, 37 ff.; P. Milyukov, *Glavniye techeniya russkoy istoricheskoy mysli* [*Main Currents of Russian Historical Thought*] (Moscow, 1898), 204–242.

[41] S. F. Platonov, *Lektsii po russkoy istorii* [*Lectures on Russian History*] (St. Petersburg, 1913), 34–35.

[42] Pypin, *Istoriya russkoy etnografii*, IV, ch. 7.

[43] N. M. Karamzin, *Pisma russkogo puteshestvennika* [*Letters of a Russian Traveler*] (2d ed., 2 vols.; Moscow, 1846); *Briefe eines reisenden Russen* (6 vols. in 3; Leipzig, 1801–1803); *Travels from Moscow, through Prussia, Germany, Switzerland, France and England*, translated from the German (3 vols.; London, 1803); *Lettres d'un voyageur russe en France, en Allemagne et en Suisse (1789–1790)* (Paris, 1867).

[44] M. Pogodin, *N. M. Karamzin, po ego sochineniyam, pismam i otzyvam sovremennikov* [*N. M. Karamzin, as Revealed in His Works and Letters and in the Opinions of His Contemporaries*] (Moscow, 1866), I, 139–144.

Notes

[45] V. V. Sipovsky, N. M. Karamzin, avtor "Pisem russkogo puteshestvennika" [N. M. Karamzin, Author of "Letters of a Russian Traveler"] (St. Petersburg, 1899), 416–417; Russkaya Mysl', VII (1891), 22–23. See also Starina i Novizna, I, 60; Pisma N. M. Karamzina k I. I. Dmitrievu] [Letters of N. M. Karamzin to I. I. Dmitriev] (St. Petersburg, 1866), 248–249.

[46] Pypin, Istoriya russkoy literatury [History of Russian Literature] (St. Petersburg, 1913), IV, 222–223; Koyalovich, op. cit., 143; Pogodin, op. cit., II, 1–2.

[47] Karamzin, Istoricheskoye pokhvalnoye slovo Ekaterine Vtoroy [A Historical Word of Praise for Catherine II] (Moscow, 1802).

[48] Pogodin, op. cit., I, 396–397.

[49] Karamzin, Istoriya gosudarstva rossiyskogo [History of the Russian State] (12 vols.; St. Petersburg, 1816–1829. Another edition, Moscow, 1903). French translation by St.-Thomas and Jauffret (11 vols.; Paris, 1819–1826). German translation (11 vols.; Riga, 1820–1833).

[50] Pogodin, op. cit., II, 2.

[51] Zhurnal ministerstva narodnogo prosvyeshcheniya, CXXXIV (1867), 20 ff.

[52] Chteniya v Imperatorskom obshchestve istorii i drevnostey rossiyskikh pri Moskovskom universitete, III (1862), 23.

[53] Zhurnal ministerstva narodnogo prosvyeshcheniya, CXXXIII (1867), 17–18.

[54] Compare the different views of Professor M. I. Koyalovich, Istoriya russkogo samosoznaniya, 143 ff., and of Professor P. N. Milyukov, Glavniye techeniya russkoy istoricheskoy mysli, 152 ff.

[55] Milyukov, op. cit., 161–163; also 187–190.

[56] Karamzin, Istoriya gosudarstva rossiyskogo (St. Petersburg, 1819), V, 64.

[57] Pypin, Istoriya russkoy literatury, IV, 224.

[58] Russky istorichesky zhurnal, I (1917), 14.

[59] Zhurnal ministerstva narodnogo prosvyeshcheniya, CXXXIII (1867), 47.

[60] N. Barsukov, Zhizn i trudy M. P. Pogodina [The Life and Works of M. P. Pogodin] (St. Petersburg, 1889), II, 333. See also E. Kovalevsky, Graf Bludov i ego vremya [Count Bludov and His Times] (St. Petersburg, 1866), 232; Dekabrist N. I. Turgenev. Pisma k bratu S. I. Turgenevu [The Decembrist N. I. Turgenev. Letters to His Brother S. I. Turgenev] (Moscow, 1936), 349.

[61] A. Borozdin, "Zhurnalist dvadtsatykh godov [A Journalist of the 'Twenties]," Istorichesky vyestnik, LXIII (1896), 946–959. Interesting material may

also be found in M. I. Sukhomlinov's *Issledovaniya i stati* [*Studies and Essays*] (St. Petersburg, 1889), II, 367–431.

[62] N. A. Polevoy, *Istoriya russkogo naroda* [*A History of the Russian People*] (6 vols.; Moscow, 1830–1833); *Istoriya Petra Velikogo* [*A History of Peter the Great*] (2d ed.; Moscow, 1899).

[63] Pypin, *Istoriya russkoy literatury*, IV, 471–472.

[64] *Istorichesky vyestnik*, LXIII (1896), 958; *Russky biograficheskly slovar*, XIV, 299–300.

[65] M. P. Pogodin, *Issledovaniya, zamechaniya i lektsii* [*Investigations, Annotations, and Lectures*] (7 vols.; Moscow, 1846–1850); *Drevnyaya russkaya istoriya do mongolskogo iga* [*Early Russian History to the Time of the Mongolian Yoke*] (3 vols.; Moscow, 1871); *Nestor: eine historisch-kritische Untersuchung über den Anfang der russischen Chroniken*, tr. by F. Löwe (St. Petersburg, 1844); *N. M. Karamzin, po ego sochineniyam, pismam i otzyvam sovremennikov* [*N. M. Karamzin, as Revealed in His Works and Letters and in the Opinions of His Contemporaries*] (2 vols.; Moscow, 1866).

[66] Bestuzhev-Ryumin, *op. cit.*, 235–236, 239–240.

[67] *Entsiklopedichesky slovar* (Brokhaus-Efron), XXIV (1), 32.

[68] *Russky biograficheskly slovar*, XIV, 159–160.

[69] See Barsukov, *op. cit.*, IV, 252–253.

[70] P. Y. Chaadayev, *Sochineniya i pisma* [*Works and Letters*] (2 vols.; Moscow, 1913–1914).

[71] Chaadayev, *op. cit.*, I, 6–7.

[72] See particularly the notable collection of folklore compiled by Peter Kireyevsky and edited by the Moscow Society of Admirers of the Russian Language, in ten volumes: *Pyesni, sobranniye P. V. Kireyevskim* [*Songs Collected by P. V. Kireyevsky*] (10 vols.; Moscow, 1868–1874).

[73] V. O. Klyuchevsky, *Ocherki i ryechi* [*Studies and Addresses*] (Moscow, n. d.), 2–3; M. N. Pokrovsky, *Borba klassov i russkaya istoricheskaya literatura* [*The Class Struggle in Russian Historical Literature*] (Petrograd, 1923), 59–60.

[74] S. M. Solovyev, *Istoriya Rossii s drevneyshikh vremyen* [*History of Russia from the Earliest Times*] (29 vols.; St. Petersburg, 1897); *Histoire de Russie*, a translation of the abridged one-volume edition (Paris, 1879); *Geschichte des Falles von Polen*, tr. by J. Spörer (Gotha, 1865); *Imperator Aleksandr I. Politika-diplomatiya* [*Politics and Diplomacy in the Reign of Alexander I*] (St. Petersburg, 1877).

[75] *Russky biograficheskly slovar*, XIX, 85, 86.

[76] E. Shmurlo, "S. M. Solovyev," *Entsiklopedichesky slovar* (Brokhaus-Efron), XXX (2), 798–803.

[77] V. O. Klyuchevsky, *Ocherki i ryechi*, 39.

[78] K. D. Kavelin, *Sobraniye sochineny* [*Collected Works*] (4 vols.; St. Petersburg, 1900).

[79] *Russky biograficheskyi slovar*, VIII, 364–365.

[80] Pypin, *Istoriya russkoy etnografii*, II, 19 ff.

[81] A. D. Gradovsky, *Sobraniye sochineny* [*Collected Works*] (9 vols.; St. Petersburg, 1899–1904).

[82] Klyuchevsky, *Opyty i issledovaniya* [*Essays and Studies*] (Moscow, 1915), 1 ff.

[83] V. O. Klyuchevsky. *Kharakteristiki i vospominaniya* [*V. O. Klyuchevsky. Essays and Recollections*] (Moscow, 1912), 13–14.

[84] Published in *Ocherki i ryechi*, 57–89; 117–139; 279–311.

[85] V. O. Klyuchevsky. *Kharakteristiki i vospominaniya*, 20–21, 22.

[86] V. O. Klyuchevsky, *Kurs russkoy istorii* [*A Course in Russian History*] (5 vols.; 1904–1921; trans. by C. J. Hogarth [London, 1911–1931]); *Istoriya soslovy v Rossii* [*A History of Classes in Russia*] (Moscow, 1913); *Boyarskaya duma drevney Rusi* [*The Boyar Council of Early Russia*] (Moscow, 1883); *Ocherki i ryechi* [*Studies and Addresses*] (Moscow, n.d.); *Opyty i issledovaniya* [*Essays and Studies*] (Moscow, 1915); *Otzyvy i otvyety* [*Reviews and Replies*] (Moscow, 1914).

[87] *Russky istorichesky zhurnal*, VIII (1922), 184–185.

[88] F. I. Shalyapin (Chaliapin), *Pages from My Life* (New York, 1927), 194–195.

[89] *Russky istorichesky zhurnal*, VIII (1922), 204 ff. See also the two exquisite essays on this subject in V. O. Klyuchevsky. *Kharakteristiki i vospominaniya*, 45–58; 59–93.

[90] Klyuchevsky, *Opyty i issledovaniya*, 212–310.

[91] See *Sbornik statey, posvyashchennykh S. F. Platonovu* (St. Petersburg, 1912), 299. Note also Klyuchevsky, *Opyty i issledovaniya*, 417 ff.

[92] Klyuchevsky, *History of Russia*, IV, chs. iii–vi, x. See also his interpretation of Catherine's reign in *Ocherki i ryechi*, 312–385.

[93] See the most recent appraisal of Klyuchevsky by G. Fedotov in *Sovremenniye zapiski* (Paris), L (1932), 340–362.

[94] K. N. Bestuzhev-Ryumin, *Biografii i kharakteristiki* [*Biographical Essays*] (St. Petersburg, 1882); *Russkaya istoriya* [*Russian History*] (2 vols.;

114 *Modern Russian Historiography*

St. Petersburg, 1872–1875); *Geschichte Russlands,* tr. by T. Schiemann (Mitau, 1877); *O tom, kak roslo Moskovskoye knyazhestvo i sdelalos russkim tsarstvom* [*How the Muscovy Principality Grew and Became the Russian State*] (St. Petersburg, 1866).

[95] *Russky istorichesky zhurnal,* VIII (1922), 225–228.

[96] S. F. Platonov, *Ocherki po istorii smuty v Moskovskom gosudarstve XVI–XVII v.v.* [*Outline of the History of the Time of Troubles in the Muscovite State in the 16th and 17th Centuries*] (St. Petersburg, 1899); *Lektsii po russkoy istorii* [*Lectures on Russian History*] (St. Petersburg, 1915); *Boris Godunov* (Petrograd, 1921); *Ivan Grozny* [*Ivan the Terrible*] (Berlin, 1924); *Histoire de la Russie des origines à 1918* (Paris, 1929); *La Russie moscovite* (Paris, 1932).

[97] M. K. Lyubavsky, *Oblastnoye deleniye i mestnoye upravleniye litovskorusskogo gosudarstva* [*Provincial Division and Local Administration of the Lithuanian-Russian State*] (Moscow, 1892); *Litovsko-russky seym* [*The Lithuanian-Russian Diet*] (Moscow, 1901); *Ocherk istorii Litovsko-russkogo gosudarstva do Lublinskoy unii vklyuchitelno* [*A Study of the Lithuanian-Russian State Down to the Union of Lublin*] (Moscow, 1910); *Obrasovaniye osnovnoy gosudarstvennoy territorii velikorusskoy narodnosti* [*The Territorial Basis of the Great Russian State*) (Leningrad, 1929).

[98] A. E. Presnyakov, *Obrazovaniye velikorusskogo gosudarstva. Ocherki po istorii XIII–XV stoletii* [*The Formation of the Great Russian State. Studies in the History of the 13th–15th Centuries*] (Petrograd, 1918); *Knyazhoye pravo v drevney Rusi* [*Prince-law in Early Russia*] (St. Petersburg, 1909); *Aleksandr I* [*Alexander I*] (Petrograd, 1924); *Apogey samoderzhaviya: Nikolay I* [*The Apogee of Autocracy: Nicholas I*] (Leningrad, 1925); *14 dekabrya 1825 goda* [*December 14, 1825*] (Leningrad, 1926).

[99] *Istorik-Marksist,* XIII, 269.

[100] For a complete list of Lappo-Danilevsky's works see *Russky istorichesky zhurnal,* VI (1920), 29–41. His most important works are the following: *Organizatsiya pryamogo oblozheniya v Moskovskom gosudarstve so vremyen smuty do epokhi preobrazovany* [*The Administration of Direct Taxation in the Muscovite State from the Time of Troubles to the Period of Reforms*] (St. Petersburg, 1890); *Skifskiye drevnosti* [*Scythian Antiquities*] (St. Petersburg, 1887); *Russkiye promyshlenniye i torgoviye kompanii v pervoy polovine XVIII stoletiya* [*Russian Industrial and Trading Companies in the First Half of the 18th Century*] (St. Petersburg, 1899); *Ocherk istorii obrazovaniya glavneyshikh razryadov krestyanskogo naseleniya v Rossii* [*Outline History of the Formation of the Main Classes Within the Peasant Population of Russia*] (St. Petersburg, 1905); *Metodologiya istorii* [*The Methodology*

Notes

of History] (St. Petersburg, 1913); *Ocherk russkoy diplomatiki chastnykh aktov* [Notes on Russian Paleography of Private Acts] (Prague, 1920); "The Development of Science and Learning in Russia," in J. D. Duff, ed., *Russian Realities and Problems* (Cambridge, 1917).

[101] See *Russky istorichesky zhurnal*, VI (1920), 97 ff.

[102] P. N. Milyukov, *Gosudarstvennoye khozyaystvo v Rossii v pervoy chetverti XVIII stoletiya i reforma Petra Velikogo* [State Economy in Russia During the First Quarter of the 18th Century and the Reforms of Peter the Great] (St. Petersburg, 1892); *Glavniye techeniya russkoy istoricheskoy mysli* [Main Currents in Russian Historical Thought] (Moscow, 1898); *Ocherki po istorii russkoy kultury* [Studies in the History of Russian Culture] (3 vols.; St. Petersburg, 1896–1903; rev. ed., Paris, 1930–); *Russia and Its Crisis* (Chicago, 1905); *Iz istorii russkoy intelligentsii* [Essays on the Russian Intelligentsia] (St. Petersburg, 1902); *Le mouvement intellectuel russe*, tr. by J. W. Bienstock (Paris, 1918); *Histoire de Russie* (in collab. with Ch. Seignobos and L. Eisenmann) (3 vols.; Paris, 1932–1933); *Zhivoy Pushkin* [The Living Pushkin] (Paris, 1937).

[103] Milyukov, *Ocherki po istorii russkoy kultury*, I, 235–238.

[104] Milyukov, *Ocherki po istorii russkoy kultury*, II, 394–396.

[105] See, e.g., P. Paradizov, *Ocherki po istoriografii dekabristov* [Outlines of the Historiography of the Decembrists] (Moscow, 1929), 161 ff.

[106] Autobiographical sketches of V. I. Semevsky may be found in *Golos minuvshego*, IX–X (1917).

[107] E. N. Vodovozova, *Na zare zhizni* [At the Dawn of Life] (Moscow, 1934), II, 339 ff.

[108] See Semevsky's address delivered before the examination board, defending his master's thesis, in *Russkaya starina*, XXXIV (1882), 577–578.

[109] V. I. Semevsky, *Krestyane v tsarstvovaniye Imperatritsy Ekateriny II* [Peasants in the Reign of the Empress Catherine II] (2 vols.; St. Petersburg, 1903); *Krestyansky vopros v Rossii v XVIII i pervoy polovine XIX vyeka* [The Peasant Question in Russia in the 18th and the First Half of the 19th Century] (2 vols.; St. Petersburg, 1888); *Rabochiye na sibirskikh zolotykh promyslakh* [Laborers in the Siberian Gold-mining Industry] (2 vols.; St. Petersburg, 1898); *Politicheskiye i obshchestvenniye idei dekabristov* [Political and Social Ideas of the Decembrists] (St. Petersburg, 1909); *M. V. Butashevich-Petrashevsky i Petrashevtsy* [M. V. Butashevich-Petrashevsky and His Circle] (Moscow, 1922).

[110] *Russkaya starina*, XXXIV (1882), 578–584.

[111] *Golos minuvshego*, IX–X (1917), 38.

116   *Modern Russian Historiography*

[112] S. Svatikov, "Opalnaya professura 80-kh godov [Dishonored Professors of the 80's]," *Golos minuvshego*, II, 1917.

[113] G. L. von Maurer, *Geschichte der Fronhöfe, der Bauernhöfe und der Hofverfassung in Deutschland* (4 vols.; n. p., 1862–1863).

[114] Semevsky, *Rabochiye na sibirskikh zolotykh promyslakh*, I, iii–iv ff.

[115] A. P. Shchapov, *Sochineniya* [*Works*] (3 vols.; St. Petersburg, 1906–1908); *Zemstvo i raskol* [*Zemstvo and the Schism*] (St. Petersburg, 1862); *Neizdanniye sochineniya* [*Unpublished Works*] (Kazan, 1926); *Sobraniye sochineny. Dopolnitelniy tom k izdaniyu 1906–08 g.g.* [*Collected works. Supplementary Volume to the Edition of 1906–08*], prepared by A. N. Turunov (Irkutsk, 1937).

[116] *Istorik-Marksist*, III (1927), 9–10.

[117] G. V. Plekhanov, *Sochineniya* [*Works*] (Moscow, 1923), II, 19.

[118] *Zhurnal ministerstva narodnogo prosvyeshcheniya*, IX–X (1875), 72.

[119] *Krasnyi Arkhiv*, IV, 407–410; *Russky biografichesky slovar*, XXIV, 5.

[120] Pypin, *Istoriya russkoy etnografii*, III, 365–367. Also, *Biograficheskiy slovar professorov Kievskogo universiteta* [*Biographical Dictionary of Professors of the University of Kiev*] (Kiev, 1884). The English reader is referred to an admirable article on Dragomanov by D. Doroshenko, "Mykhailo Dragomanov and the Ukrainian National Movement," *Slavonic Review*, XVI (1938), 654–666.

[121] Pypin, *Istoriya russkoy etnografii*, III, 151 ff.

[122] N. I. Kostomarov, *Istoricheskiye monografii i issledovaniya* [*Historical Monographs and Studies*] (21 vols.; St. Petersburg, 1903–1906); *Russkaya istoriya v zhizneopisaniyakh eya glavneyshikh deyateley* [*A History of Russia in Biographies of Its Leading Statesmen*] (2 vols.; St. Petersburg, 1903–1907); *Posledniye gody Rechi-Pospolitoy* [*The Closing Years of the Polish Commonwealth*] (St. Petersburg, 1870); *Bunt Stenki Razina* [*The Rebellion of Stenka Razin*] (St. Petersburg, 1859).

[123] M. S. Hrushevsky, *Istoriya Ukrainy-Rusi* [*History of Ukrainian Russia*] (9 vols.; Kiev-Lwów, 1898–1928); *Zherela do istorii Ukrainy-Rusi* [*Sources Pertaining to the History of Ukrainian Russia*] (Vols. I–VIII, XII, 1895–1913; XXII, 1913; XXVI, 1924; Kiev-Lwów); *Istoriya Kievskoy zemli* [*History of Kievan Russia*] (Kiev, 1891).

[124] A detailed discussion on Siberian historiography may be found in A. N. Pypin, *Istoriya russkoy etnografii*, IV, pt. 2; also in V. I. Ogorodnikov, *Ocherk istorii Sibiri* [*Outline History of Siberia*], 1–92.

[125] See Pekarsky, *Istoriya Akademii Nauk*, I, 366–368, 427.

[126] G. F. Müller, *Opisaniye sibirskogo tsarstva* [*A Description of the Siberian Kingdom*] (St. Petersburg, 1750; 2d ed., 1787); *Sammlung russischer Geschichte* (9 vols.; St. Petersburg, 1732–1764; Vol. X, Dorpat, 1816).

[127] P. A. Slovtsov, *Istoricheskoye obozreniye Sibiri* [*A Historical Survey of Siberia*] (2 vols.; St. Petersburg, 1838–1844).

[128] I. V. Shcheglov, *Khronologichesky perechen vazhneyshikh dannykh iz istorii Sibiri (1032–1882)* [*Chronological List of the Most Important Events in the History of Siberia, 1032–1882*] (Irkutsk, 1883).

[129] V. K. Andrievich, *Istoriya Sibiri* [*History of Siberia*] (5 vols. in 2; St. Petersburg, 1889).

[130] P. N. Butsinsky, *Zaseleniye Sibiri i byt pervykh eya naselnikov* [*The Settlement of Siberia and the Life of Its First Settlers*] (Kharkov, 1869); *K istorii Sibiri: Surgut, Narym i Ketsk do 1645 goda* [*Notes on the History of Siberia: Surgut, Narym, and Ketsk to 1645*] (Kharkov, 1893); *Mangazeya i Mangazeysky uyezd (1601–1645 g.g.)* [*Mangazeya and Mangazeysk County, 1601–1645*] (Kharkov, 1893).

[131] P. M. Golovachev, *Rossiya na Dalnem Vostokè* [*Russia in the Far East*] (St. Petersburg, 1904); N. M. Yadrintsev, *Sibir kak koloniya* [*Siberia as a Colony*] (St. Petersburg, 1892).

[132] N. N. Ogloblin, *Obozreniye stolbtsov i knig sibirskogo prikaza 1592–1768 g.g.* [*A Survey of the Rolls and Books of the Siberian Prikaz, 1592–1768*] (4 vols.; Moscow, 1859–1900).

[133] V. I. Vaghin, *Istoricheskiye svedeniya o deyatelnosti gr. M. M. Speranskogo v Sibiri s 1819 po 1822 god* [*Historical Data on the Activity of Count M. M. Speransky in Siberia from 1819 to 1822*] (2 vols.; St. Petersburg, 1872); S. M. Prutchenko, *Sibirskiye okrainy* [*Siberian Borderlands*] (2 vols.; St. Petersburg, 1899).

[134] J. P. Barsukov, *Graf N. N. Muravyev-Amursky* [*Count N. N. Muravyev-Amursky*] (2 vols.; Moscow, 1891).

[135] P. Tikhmenev, *Istoricheskoye obozreniye obrazovaniya Rossiysko-amerikanskoy kompanii i deystvy eya do nastoyashchego vremeni* [*A Historical Survey of the Formation of the Russian-American Company and Its History to the Present Time*] (2 vols.; St. Petersburg, 1861–1863).

[136] N. N. Firsov, *Chteniya po istorii Sibiri* [*Readings in the History of Siberia*] (2 vols.; Moscow, 1920–1921); *Polozheniye inorodtsev severo-vostochnoy Rossii v Moskovskom gosudarstve* [*Position of the Natives of Northeastern Russia in the Muscovite State*] (Kazan, 1866).

[137] S. V. Bakhrushin, *Kazaki na Amure* [*Cossacks on the Amur*] (Leningrad, 1925); *Ocherki po istorii Sibiri v XVI i XVII v. v.* [*Outline History*

of the Colonization of Siberia in the 16th and 17th Centuries] (Moscow, 1927); *Pokruta na sobolinnykh promyslakh semnadtsatogo vyeka* [*Contracts in the Sable Trade in the Seventeenth Century*] (n. p., n. d.); "Sibirskie sluzhiliye tatary v XVII veke [Siberian Tartar Vassals in the 17th Century]," *Istoricheskie zapiski* (Moscow), I (1937), 55–80.

[138] V. I. Ogorodnikov, *Ocherk istorii Sibiri do nachala XIX stolyetiya. Vvedeniye. Istoriya do russkoy Sibiri* [*An Outline of Siberian History to the 19th Century. Introduction: History to the Russian Conquest*] (Irkutsk, 1920); *Zavoevaniye russkimi Sibiri* [*The Conquest of Siberia by the Russians*] (Vladivostok, 1924); *Russkaya gosudarstvennaya vlast i sibirskiye inorodtsy v XVI–XVII v. v.* [*Russian Administration and the Siberian Natives in the 16th–17th Centuries*] (Irkutsk, 1920); *Iz istorii pokoreniya Sibiri. Pokoreniye Yukagirskoy zemli* [*History of the Conquest of Siberia. Conquest of the Yukagir Territory*] (Chita, 1922); *Tuzemnoye i russkoye zemledeliye na Amure v XVIII vyeke* [*Native and Russian Farming in the Amur District in the 18th Century*] (Vladivostok, 1927).

[139] *Russky istorichesky zhurnal*, VII (1921), 114–120.

[140] A. A. Shakhmatov, *Rozyskaniya o drevneyshikh letopisnykh svodakh* [*Investigations Pertaining to the Earliest Chronicles*] (St. Petersburg, 1903); *O yazyke novgorodskikh gramot* [*The Language of the Novgorodian Charters*] (St. Petersburg, 1885); *Issledovaniye o Dvinskikh gramotakh* [*A Study of the Dvinsk Charters*] (St. Petersburg, 1903); *Nyeskolko zamyetok o yazyke Pskovskikh pyamyatnikov* [*A Few Notes on the Language of the Pskov Records*] (St. Petersburg, 1909); *Ocherk drevneyshogo perioda istorii russkogo literaturnogo yazyka* [*A Study of the Modern Russian Literary Language*] (St. Petersburg, 1915); *Vvedeniye v kurs istorii russkogo yazyka* [*Introduction to the History of the Russian Language*] (Petrograd, 1916); *Drevneyshiye sud'by russkogo plemeni* [*Earliest Fate of the Russian Tribes*] (Petrograd, 1919). See also *Povest' vremennykh lyet* [*Annals of Ancient Times*], tr. by R. Trautmann (Leipzig, 1931), and Samuel H. Cross, *The Russian Primary Chronicle* (Cambridge, Mass., 1930).

[141] V. S. Ikonnikov, *Opyt russkoy istoriografii* [*A Study of Russian Historiography*] (2 vols. in 4; Kiev, 1891–1908); *Graf N. S. Mordvinov* [*Count N. S. Mordvinov*] (St. Petersburg, 1873); "Krestyanskoye dvizheniye v Kievskoy gubernii v 1826–27 g.g. v svyazi s sobytiyami togo vremeni [The Peasant Movement in the Kiev Government in 1826–27 in Relation to the Events of the Period]," in *Sbornik statey, posvyashchennykh V. I. Lamanskomu* (pt. 2, pp. 657–742; St. Petersburg, 1908).

[142] N. P. Pavlov-Silvansky, *Feodalizm v drevney Rusi* [*Feudalism in Early Russia*] (St. Petersburg, 1907); *Feodalizm v udelnoy Rusi* [*Feudalism in*

Appanage Russia] (St. Petersburg, 1910); *Gosudarevy-sluzhiliye lyudi: proiskhozhdeniye russkogo dvoryanstva* [*The Sovereign's Servant-men: the Origin of the Russian Nobility*] (St. Petersburg, 1898); *Dekabrist Pestel' pred verkhovnym ugolovnym sudom* [*The Decembrist Pestel Before the Supreme Criminal Court*] (Rostov, 1907). See also B. D. Grekov, *Feodalniye otnosheniya v Kievskom gosudarstve* [*Feudal Relations in the Kievan State*] (Moscow, 1935).

[143] G. V. Plekhanov, *Istoriya russkoy obshchestvennoy mysli* [*History of Russian Social Thought*], in his *Complete Works*, Vols. XX–XXII (Moscow, 1923–1927).

[144] N. A. Rozhkov, *Russkaya istoriya* [*History of Russia*] (12 vols.; Moscow, 1919–1926); *Selskoye khozyaystvo Moskovskoy Rusi XVI vyeka* [*Agrarian Economy of Muscovite Russia in the 16th Century*] (Moscow, 1899).

[145] M. N. Pokrovsky, *Russkaya istoriya s drevneyshikh vremyen* [*Russian History from the Earliest Times*] (4 vols.; Moscow, 1913–1914; latest edition, Moscow, 1932–1933); *History of Russia*, tr. by J. D. Clarkson (New York, 1931); *Brief History of Russia*, tr. by D. Mirsky (2 vols.; New York, 1933); *Diplomatiya i voyny tsarskoy Rossii v XIX stolyetii* [*The Diplomacy and Wars of Tsarist Russia in the 19th Century*] (Moscow, 1923); *Ocherki russkogo revolyutsionnogo dvizheniya XIX–XX v.v.* [*Studies of the Russian Revolutionary Movement of the 19th–20th Centuries*] (Moscow, 1924); *Ocherk istorii russkoy kultury* [*An Outline History of Russian Culture*] (2 vols.; Petrograd, 1923); *Istoricheskaya nauka i borba klassov* [*Historical Science and the Class Struggle*] (Moscow, 1933). For a complete list of Pokrovsky's works, see *Istorik-Marksist*, I–II (1932), 216–248.

[146] P. N. Milyukov, "Velichiye i padeniye M. N. Pokrovskogo [The Greatness and Decline of M. N. Pokrovsky]," *Sovremenniye zapiski* (Paris), LXV (1937), 370.

[147] *Istorik-Marksist*, I (1926), 320.

[148] *Mezhdunarodniye otnosheniya v epokhu imperializma, 1878–1917* [*International Relations During the Era of Imperialism*] (Ser. III, Vol. I–; Moscow, 1931–). There is also a German translation of this publication (Berlin, 1931–).

[149] L. Mamet, "Istoriya i obshchestvenno-politicheskoye vospitaniye [History and Social-political Education]," *Istorik-Marksist*, XIV (1929), 159 ff.

[150] *Izvestiya*, May 16, 1934.

[151] A. Pankratova, "Za bolshevistskoye prepodavaniye istorii [For a Bolshevik Teaching of History]," *Bolshevik*, XXIII (1934), 40.

[152] *Izvestiya*, July 22, 1937, p. 4.

[153] F. Gorochov, "An Anti-Marxist Theory of History," *International Literature*, IX (1937), 73.

[154] *Izvestiya akademii nauk*, O.O.N., Ser. VII, Vol. IX (1932), 782.

[155] *Vyestnik kommunisticheskoy akademii*, IV (1933), 33, 48.

[156] M. Kammari, "Teoreticheskiye korni oshibochnykh vzglyadov M. N. Pokrovskogo [Theoretical Roots of the Erroneous Historical Views of M. N. Pokrovsky]," *Pod znamenem marksizma*, IV (1936), 5–6.

[157] N. Bukharin, "Nuzhna li nam marksistskaya istoricheskaya nauka? [Do We Need a Marxist Historical Science?]," *Izvestiya*, January 27, 1936, 3–4; *Moscow News*, September 1, 1937. See also Pankratova, *op. cit.*, pp. 32–51. Stalin's own view concerning the writing of history is given in the *Istorik-Marksist*, II (1937), 29–31, and in *Krasny arkhiv*, III (82), 1937, 3–5. It is perhaps appropriate to recall a letter from Lenin to Pokrovsky, the first paragraph of which reads: "I congratulate you very heartily on your success. I like your new book 'Brief history of Russia' immensely. The construction and the narrative are original. It reads with tremendous interest. It should, in my opinion, be translated into the European languages."—M. N. Pokrovsky, *A Brief History of Russia* (tr. by D. S. Mirsky), I, 5.

[158] *Kniga i proletarskaya revolyutsiya*, X (1937), 103.

[159] *New York Times*, November 16, 1936. See also *Za kommunisticheskoye prosvyeshcheniye*, May 16, 1937.

[160] *Izvestiya*, September 15, 1937. On the latest interpretation of the adoption of Christianity in Kievan Russia and the correction of the "pseudoscientific views of Pokrovsky's school," see S. Bakhrushin, "K voprosu o kreshchenii Kievskoy Rusi," *Istorik-Marksist*, II (1937), 40, 63.

[161] E. Tarlé, *Nashestviye Napoleona na Rossiyu, 1812 god*. [*The Invasion of Russia by Napoleon, 1812*] (Moscow, 1938). *Za kommunisticheskoye prosvyeshcheniye*, February 14, 1937. Note also *Izvestiya*, August 22 and 24, 1937; *Bolshevik*, XVIII (1937), 39 ff.

[162] *Izvestiya*, August 24, 1937, p. 2. Cf. Pokrovsky, *Russkaya istoriya* (ed. 1933), II, 236 ff.; 300–302.

[163] *Kratky kurs istorii SSSR* [*A Brief Course in the History of the USSR*], ed. by Professor A. V. Shestakov (Moscow, 1937). The opening paragraph of this textbook reads as follows: "The USSR is the land of socialism. There is only one socialist country on the globe—it is our motherland." And the closing paragraph of the Introduction chants: "We love our motherland and we must know well her wonderful history. Whoever knows history will better understand current life, will fight better the enemies of our country, and will consolidate socialism."

Notes   121

[164] The complete text of the decision may be found in *Izvestiya*, August 22, 1937, p. 2. Also P. Drozdov, " 'Istoricheskaya shkola' Pokrovskogo [The 'Historical School' of Pokrovsky];' *Pravda*, March 28, 1937, pp. 2-3.

[165] Cf. Pokrovsky's interpretations in *Russkaya istoriya* (ed. 1933), II, 153-154, 160, 168; *Diplomatiya i voyny tsarskoy Rossii v XIX stolyetii* [*The Diplomacy and Wars of Tsarist Russia in the 19th Century*], passim.

[166] An able discussion of Soviet historiographic problems may be found in B. H. Sumner, "Soviet History," *Slavonic Review*, XVI (1938), 601-615.

[167] See an early account of *émigré* publications discussed in *Russkaya zarubezhnaya kniga* [*Russian Books Abroad*] (Praha, 1924), I, 66-95.

[168] M. I. Rostovtsev, *Iranians and Greeks in South Russia* (Oxford, 1922); *Skythien und der Bosporus* (Berlin, 1931); *Sredinnaya Aziya, Rossiya, Kitai i zveriniy stil* [*Central Asia, Russia, China, and the Animal Style*] (Prague, Seminarium Kondakovium, 1929).

[169] G. V. Vernadsky, *La charte constitutionelle de l'empire russe de l'an 1820* (Paris, 1933).

[170] V. V. Bartold, *Istoriya izucheniya Vostoka v Evrope i Rossii* [*A Historical Study of the East in Europe and in Russia*] (2d ed.; Leningrad, 1925). See I. Y. Krachkovsky, "V. V. Bartold v istorii islamovedeniya [V. V. Bartold in the History of Islamic Study];' *Izvestiya Akademii Nauk, O. O. N.*, Ser. VII, Vol. I (1934), 5-18.

[171] P. N. Savitsky (Savickij), "Evraziyskaya kontseptsiya russkoy geografii [The Eurasian Conception of Russian Geography];' *Zbornik radova na III Kongresu slovenskih geografa i etnografa v Yugoslavji*, 1930, 13-14.

[172] G. V. Vernadsky, *Nachertaniye russkoy istorii* [*An Outline of Russian History*] (Prague, 1927); *A History of Russia* (New Haven, 1930); *Opyt istorii Evrazii s poloviny VI vyeka do nastoyashchego vremeni* [*Essay on the History of Eurasia from the Middle of the 6th Century to the Present Time*] (Berlin, 1934); *Political and Diplomatic History of Russia* (Boston, 1936); *Zvenya russkoy kultury* [*Links in Russian Culture*] (n. p., 1938). Vol. I, *Ancient Rus'*. (This last is a projected four-volume work.)

[173] See I. R——, *Naslediye Chingiskhana* [*The Legacy of Genghis Khan*] (Berlin, 1925). It may be noted that the views of the Eurasians coincide with those of Pokrovsky in some respects. See Pokrovsky, *Istoricheskaya nauka i borba klassov* [*Historical Science and the Class Struggle*], II, 307.

[174] Vernadsky, *Opyt istorii Evrazii* [*Essay on the History of Eurasia*], 7-8.

[175] P. N. Savitsky (Savickij), *Geograficheskiye osobennosti Rossii* [*Geographical Characteristics of Russia*] (Prague, 1927); *Rossiya osobyi geografichesky mir* [*Russia as a Distinct Geographical Entity*] (Prague, 1927); *Šestína svĕta*

(Prague, 1933). Other important Eurasian literature: Prince N. S. Trubetskoy, *K probleme russkogo samopoznaniya* [*Contributions to the Problem of Russian Self-realization*] (Paris, 1931); P. O. Yakobson, *K kharakteristike evraziyskogo soyuza* [*Descriptive Notes on the Eurasian Linguistic Union*] (Paris, 1931); N. N. Alekseyev, *Teoriya gosudarstva* [*The Theory of the State*] (Paris, 1931).

[176] Milyukov, *Ocherki po istorii russkoy kultury* (rev. ed.; Paris, 1937), I (1), 35, 36.

[177] The Eurasian school has been subjected to severe criticism by Paul Milyukov. See his essay, "Eurasianism and Europeanism in Russian History," *Festschrift Th. G. Masaryk zum 80. Geburtstage* (Supplement to *Der russische Gedanke*) (Bonn, 1930), I, 225–236.

[178] For further exposition of the Eurasian philosophy, and its conception of state, church, and nation, see the admirable summary by D. S. Mirsky, "The Eurasian Movement," *Slavonic Review*, December, 1927, 311–319; "Histoire d'une émancipation," *Nouvelle Revue Française*, September, 1931, 384–397.

GENERAL BIBLIOGRAPHY

Books

BESTUZHEV-RYUMIN, K. N. *Biografii i kharakteristiki* [*Biographical Essays*]. St. Petersburg, 1882.

DOROSHENKO, D. *Oglyad ukrainskoy istoriografii* [*A Survey of Ukrainian Historiography*]. Prague, 1923.

DOVNAR-ZAPOLSKY, M. *Iz istorii obshchestvennykh techeny v Rossii* [*A History of Social Movements in Russia*]. Kiev, 1905. (See pp. 232–267.)

Entsiklopedichesky Slovar [*Russian Encyclopedia*]. St. Petersburg, Brockhaus-Efron, 1890–1904. 41 vols.

GAPANOVICH, I. *Russian Historiography Outside of Russia*. Peiping, 1935.

HECKER, JULIUS F. *Russian Sociology*. New York, 1934.

Histoire et historiens depuis cinquante ans: méthodes, organisation et résultats du travail historique de 1876 à 1926. Paris, Bibliothèque de la Revue Historique, 1927. (See Vol. I, pp. 341–370.)

IKONNIKOV, V. S. *Opyt russkoy istoriografii* [*A Study of Russian Historiography*]. Kiev, 1891–1908. 2 vols. in 4.

Klyuchevsky, V. O. [In memoriam.] *Kharakteristiki i vospominaniya* [*Essays and Recollections*]. Moscow, 1912.

KLYUCHEVSKY, V. O. *Ocherki i ryechi* [*Studies and Addresses*]. Second collection of articles. Moscow, n.d.

KOYALOVICH, M. I. *Istoriya russkogo samosoznaniya* [*History of Russian Self-realization*]. St. Petersburg, 1893.

MASARYK, T. G. *The Spirit of Russia*. New York, 1919. 2 vols.

MILYUKOV, P. N. *Glavniye techeniya russkoy istoricheskoy mysli* [*Main Currents in Russian Historical Thought*]. Moscow, 1898.

MILYUKOV, P. N. *Le mouvement intellectuel russe*. Paris, 1918.

PLATONOV, F. S. *Lektsii po russkoy istorii* [*Lectures on Russian History*]. St. Petersburg, 1915. (See the introductory chapter.)

POKROVSKY, M. N. *Borba klassov i russkaya istoricheskaya literatura* [*The Class Struggle in Russian Historical Literature*]. Petrograd, "Priboy," 1923.

POKROVSKY, M. N. *Russkaya istoricheskaya literatura v klassovom osvyeshchenii* [*A Class Interpretation of Russian Historical Literature*]. Moscow, 1927–1930. 2 vols.

PYPIN, A. N. *Istoriya russkoy etnografii* [*History of Russian Ethnography*]. St. Petersburg, 1890–1892. 4 vols.

SHAKHNAZAROV, I. D. *Russkoye revolyutsionnoye prosvyeshcheniye v borbe s burzhuazno-dvoryanskoy istoriografiey* [*Russian Revolutionary Education in Its Conflict with Bourgeois-Gentry Historiography*]. Leningrad, Academy of Sciences, 1934. Also in *Problemy Marksizma*, V, 1933, 48–73.

Articles

"Arkhiv Semevskogo [The Archive of Semevsky]." *Literaturnoye naslyedstvo,* VII–VIII, 418–430.

Azadovsky, M. "Zadachi Sibirskoy bibliografii [Problems of Siberian Bibliography]." *Sibirskiye zapiski,* VI, 1919.

Bakhrushin, S. V. "Müller kak istorik Sibiri [Müller as a Historian of Siberia]." In Müller's latest edition of *Istoriya Sibiri* [*History of Siberia*], published in 1937 by the Academy of Sciences, 5–55.

Bidlo, Jaroslav. "Remarques à la défense de ma conception de l'histoire de l'orient Européen et de l'histoire des peuples slaves." *Bulletin d'Information des Sciences Historiques en Europe Orientale,* VI, fasc. 3–4. Varsovie, 1934. Cf. Derzhavin, N., "Iz itogov VII mezhdunarodnogo kongressa istoricheskikh nauk v Varshave [Observations on the 7th International Congress of Historical Sciences in Warsaw]." *Trudy instituta slavyanovedeniya Akademii Nauk SSSR,* II (1934), 475–482.

Epstein, F. "Die marxistische Geschichtswissenschaft in der Sovjetunion seit 1927." *Jahrbücher für Kultur und Geschichte der Slaven,* VI, 1 (1930).

Fedotov, G. "Rossiya Klyuchevskogo [Klyuchevsky's Russia]." *Sovremenniye zapiski,* L (1932), 340–362.

Florovsky, A. "La littérature historique russe-émigration." *Bulletin d'Information des Sciences Historiques en Europe Orientale* (Varsovie), I, 82–121; III, 25–79.

Florovsky, A. "Russkaya istoricheskaya nauka v emigratsii [Russian Historical Science in Emigration]." *Trudy V-go S'yezda russkikh akademicheskikh organizatsy za-granitsey* (Belgrade), I (1931).

Florovsky, A. "The Works of Russian *Emigrés* in History (1921–1927)." *Slavonic Review,* VII (1928), 216–219.

Gautier, G. "Histoire de Russie: publications des années 1917–1927." *Revue Historique,* CLVII (1928), 93–123.

Golubtsov, S. A. "Teoreticheskiye vzglyady V. O. Klyuchevskogo [Theoretical views of Klyuchevsky]." *Russky istorichesky zhurnal,* VIII (1922), 178–202.

Gorin, P. "M. N. Pokrovsky—bolshevik-istorik [M. N. Pokrovsky—Bolshevik Historian]." *Vyestnik kommunisticheskoy akademii,* IV (1933), 42–48.

Gurko-Kryazhin, B. "M. N. Pokrovsky i izucheniye istorii Vostoka [M. N. Pokrovsky and the Study of the History of the Orient]." *Novy vostok,* XXV (1929), 29–46.

Hrushevsky, M. S. "Ob ukrainskoy istoriografii XVIII vyeka. Neskolko soobrazheny [A Few Reflections on Ukrainian Historiography of the 18th Century]." *Izvestiya akademii nauk, O.O.N.,* Ser. VII, Vol. III (1934), 215–223.

JONAS, HANS. "Die Entwicklung der Geschichtsforschung in der Sovjet-Union seit dem Ausgang des Weltkrieges." *Zeitschrift für osteuropäische Geschichte,* V (1931), 66–83; 386–396.

KHODOROV, A. E. "M. N. Pokrovsky i izucheniye Dalnego Vostoka [M. N. Pokrovsky and the Study of the Far East]." *Novy vostok,* XXV (1929), 1–28.

KIESEWETTER (KIZEVETTER), A. "Histoire de Russie: travaux des savants russes émigrés (1918–1928)." *Revue Historique,* CLXIII (1930), 160–183.

KIESEWETTER (KIZEVETTER), A. "Karamzin." *Russky istorichesky zhurnal,* I (1917), 9–26.

KIESEWETTER (KIZEVETTER), A. "Klyuchevsky and his *Course in Russian History.*" *Slavonic Review,* I (1922), 504–522.

KORABLEV, V. N. "Akademik A. N. Pypin i slavyansky vopros [Academician A. N. Pypin and the Slav Question]." *Vyestnik akademii nauk SSSR,* VIII–IX (1933), 67–78.

LAPPO-DANILEVSKY, A. S. "The Development of Science and Learning in Russia." In *Russian Realities and Problems,* ed. by J. D. Duff (Cambridge, 1917), 153–229.

LEPPMANN, W. "Die russische Geschichtswissenschaft in der Emigration." *Zeitschrift für osteuropäische Geschichte,* V (1931), 215–248.

LUKIN, N. M. "Akademik M. N. Pokrovsky [Academician M. N. Pokrovsky]." *Izvestiya akademii nauk SSSR,* O.O.N., Ser. VII, Vol. IX (1932), 773–782.

MAKLAKOV, B. "Klyuchevsky." *Slavonic Review,* XIII (1935), 320–329.

MAZOUR, ANATOLE G. "Modern Russian Historiography." *Journal of Modern History,* IX (1937), 169–202.

MILYUKOV, P. "Eurasianism and Europeanism in Russian History." *Festschrift T. G. Masaryk zum 80. Geburtstage* (Supplement to *Der russische Gedanke,* Bonn), I (1930), 225–236.

MILYUKOV, P. "Velichiye i padeniye M. N. Pokrovskogo [The Greatness and Decline of M. N. Pokrovsky]." *Sovremenniye zapiski* (Paris), LXV (1937), 368–387.

"Neskolko dokumentov iz tsarskikh arkhivov o M. N. Pokrovskom [Several Documents from Tsarist Archives Concerning M. N. Pokrovsky]." *Krasny arkhiv,* III (1932), 5–53.

NEVSKY, V. M. "M. N. Pokrovsky–istorik oktyabrya [M. N. Pokrovsky–Historian of the October Revolution]." *Istoriya proletariata SSSR,* XII (1932), 3–20.

PFITZNER, J. "Die Geschichte Osteuropas und die Geschichte des Slawentums als Forschungsprobleme." *Historische Zeitschrift,* Bd. 150 (1934), 21–85.

PIKSANOV, N. K. "Akademik A. N. Pypin [Academician A. N. Pypin]." *Vyestnik akademii nauk SSSR,* IV (1933), 39–44.

PIONTKOVSKY, S. "Velikoderzhavniye tendentsii v istoriografii Rossii [Autocratic Tendencies in Russian Historiography]." *Istorik-Marksist*, XVII (1930), 21–26.
PIONTKOVSKY, S. "Velikorusskaya burzhuaznaya istoriografiya poslednego desyatiletiya [Great-Russian Bourgeois Historiography of the Last Decade]." *Istorik-Marksist*, XVIII–XIX (1930), 157–176.
POKROVSKY, M. N. " 'Noviye' techeniya v russkoy istoricheskoy literature ['New' Currents in Russian Historical Literature]." *Istorik-Marksist*, VII (1928), 1–17.
PRESNYAKOV, A. E. "V. O. Klyuchevsky." *Russky istorichesky zhurnal*, VIII (1922), 203–224.
RUBINSHTEIN, N. "M. N. Pokrovsky—istorik vneshney politiki" [M. N. Pokrovsky—Historian of Foreign Policy]." *Istorik-Marksist*, IX (1928), 58–78.
SHCHEGLOV, A. "Metodologicheskiye istoki oshibok M. N. Pokrovskogo. [Methodological Sources of the Errors of M. N. Pokrovsky]." *Pod znamenem marksizma*, V (1936), 55–69.
SKUBITSKY, T. "Klassovaya borba v ukrainskoy istoricheskoy literature [The Class Struggle in Ukrainian Historical Literature]." *Istorik-Marksist*, XVII (1930), 27–40.
STRUVE, P. "Ivan Aksakov." *Slavonic Review*, II (1924), 514–518.
SUKHOTIN, L. M. "Kratky ocherk russkoy istoriografii [A Brief Outline of the Development of Russian Historiography]." *Sbornik arkheologicheskogo obshchestva* (Belgrade) (1927), 61–76.
TOMPKINS, S. R. "Trends in Communist Historical Thought." *Slavonic Review*, XIII (1935), 294–319.
"Uebersicht der historischen Literatur Russlands für die Jahre 1860–1865." *Historische Zeitschrift*, XVI, 126–174.
YUGOV, M. "Polozheniye i zadachi istoricheskogo fronta v Belorussii [The Situation and Problems Concerning the Historical Front in White Russia]." *Istorik-Marksist*, XVII, 41–50.

INDEX

Academy of Sciences, 4, 9, 20, 21, 51, 53, 58, 59, 83
Adrianov, A. V., 78
Aksakov, 34, 35
Alexander I, 10, 18, 23, 56
Alexander II, 65
"Amateur school," 13, 75
Andrievich, Major General V. K., 77
Antonovich, V. B., 68, 70, 103
Archeographical Commission, 5–6, 21, 76, 81, 105

Bagrov, L. G., 99
Bakhrushin, S. V., 79
Bakunin, 71
Bantysh-Kamensky, N. N., 8
Barskov, Y., 47
Bartold, V. V., 100
Barsukov, I. P., 78
Bayer, G. S., 5, 17
Belinsky, 34
Belyayev, I., 35, 62
Betskoy, I. I., 59
Bestuzhev-Ryumin, K. N., 51–52, 54, 64, 65, 69
Bodin, 14
Bogdanovich, 67
Bogolovsky, Professor M. M., 60, 105
Boltin, Major General Ivan N., 11, 13–15, 17
Buckle, Henry T., 49, 52, 68
Butsinsky, Professor P. N., 77–78
Byedniy, Demyan, 91

Catherine II, 7, 12, 13, 14, 23, 24, 59
Central Committee of the Communist Party, 87, 91; decree of, 87–88
Chaadayev, P. Y., 33, 60
Chasles, Victor, 37
Chernyshevsky, 69

Chicherin, B., 35, 42, 48, 49, 55, 57, 62
Chronicle of Nestor, 10, 15, 18, 25, 27, 81
Comte, 59
Council of the People's Commissars, 86; decree of, 87–88

Democratic Panslavist Cyril-Methodius Society, 71–72
Dmitriyev, 35
Dobrovsky, Abbot Joseph, 81
Dostoyevsky, 51
Dovnar-Zapolsky, 67
Dragomanov, M. P., 68, 70, 71, 103
Dyakonov, 43, 62

Efimenko, Mme., 63
Eichhorn, 41
Engelmann, J., 49
Eurasian school, 99–104 *passim*
Ewers, J. P. G., 10, 37

"Federal school," 68, 103; Ukrainian, 71
Federalists, 70, 73
Filippov, 43
Firsov, Professor N. N., 79
Fischer, Johann, 75
Florovsky, A. V., 99
Fonvizin, 46
Friedland, 95

German school, 17, 41, 52
Golovachev, P. M., 78
Goltsev, V. A., 67
Gradovsky, A. D., 43, 57
Granovsky, 34, 36, 51
Grekov, B. D., 62, 83
Guizot, 29, 37

[127]

Index

Hegel, 35, 39, 59
Hegelianism, 47
Herzen, 32, 34, 71
"Historico-juridical school," 43
Hrushevsky, M. S., 25, 68, 73–75, 82, 105

Ikonnikov, V. S., 53, 78, 81–82
Ivan IV, 52, 53
Ivan the Terrible, 48, 50
Ivanov, G., 44

"Juridical" school, 57

Kachenovsky, M., 28, 32
Kant, 35
Karamzin, N. M., 1, 12, 18, 22–29, 30, 37, 51, 68
Kareyev, 63
Karpovich, M. M., 99
Kavelin, K. D., 35, 41–44, 71
Khmelnitsky, Bogdan, 94
Khodsky, 62
Khomyakov, 34
Kireyevsky brothers, 34
Klyuchevsky, V. O., 40, 41, 43, 44–51, 52, 53, 54, 55, 57, 59, 60, 65, 82, 83, 84, 101, 105
Kondakov Institute, Czechoslovakia, 98
Korkunov, 43
Kornilov, 62
Kostomarov, N. I., 43, 68, 71–72, 73, 105
Kovalevsky, M. M., 67
Kuznetsov, I., 77

Lappo, I. I., 43, 99
Lappo-Danilevsky, A. S., 57–59, 62
Latkin, 43
Le Clerc, N. G., 13, 14
"Legal Marxists," 90

Lenin, 90, 91
Lenormand, 37
Lermontov, 46
Lomonosov, 9, 16
Luchitsky, 63
Lurye, M., 95
Lyubavsky, Professor M. K., 43, 54–55, 85, 105

Malinovsky, A., 26
Martens, F., 44
Marxian school, 83, 84, 89, 91
Marxism, 84, 90
Marxist Historical Society, 86
Maurer, G. L. von, 66
Mechnikov, 64
Michelet, 37
Mickiewicz, Adam, 37
Miller, O. F., 67
Milyukov, Professor P. N., 27, 57, 59–62, 82, 83, 101, 104, 105, 106
Minin, 92
Montesquieu, 14
Mordvinov, Count N. S., 82
Moscow Archeological: Society, 46; Institute, 79
Moscow Society of History and Russian Antiquities, 18, 19
Müller, G. F., 4, 5–8, 9, 10, 14, 15, 16, 17, 75, 76
Muravyev, M., 26
Muravyev, N., 28
Muravyev-Amursky, Count, 78
Muromtsev, S. A., 67
Musin-Pushkin, Count A. I., 13
Myakotin, V. A., 62, 99

Neander, August, 37
Nicholas I, 32, 56, 77
Niebuhr, B. G., 24, 28, 29, 41
Nolde, 43
Novikov, N. I., 22

Index

Odinets, D. N., 99
Ogloblin, N. N., 78
Ogorodnikov, V. I., 79
Oksenov, A. V., 78
Oksman, 95

Pankratova, A., 88
Pavlov-Silvansky, N. P., 82–83
Perfetsky, E. Y., 99
Peter I (the Great), 3, 11, 13, 14, 23, 33, 34, 48, 50, 59, 60, 62, 93, 95
Piontkovsky, 95
Platonov, S. F., 51, 52–53, 54, 85, 105
Plekhanov, G. V., 83, 84
Pogodin, A. L., 99
Pogodin, N. P., 28, 30–32, 36, 38, 51, 82
Pokrovsky, M. N., 83–86, 89, 90, 91, 95, 105, 106
Polevoy, N. A., 28, 29–30, 32, 92
Pososhkov, Ivan, 69
Pozharsky, 92
Presnyakov, A. E., 54, 55–57, 105
Prutchenko, S. M., 78
Pushkin, 26, 29, 46, 51, 60
Pypin, A. N., 35, 67

Quinet, Edgar, 37

Ranke, 39, 41
Romanovich-Slavatinsky, 43
Rostovtsev, M. I., 63, 99
Rozhkov, N. A., 84
Rumyantsev, Count N. P., 19, 20, 22, 26
Russian-American Company, 79
Russian Archeological Society, Yugoslavia, 98
Russian Geographical Society, 76
Russian Historical Society, Czechoslovakia, 98

Šafařík, 37
Samarin, 34
Savigny, 41
Savitsky, P. N., 101, 103
Schelling, 35, 60
Schlözer, A. L. von, 1, 7, 8–11, 12, 14, 15, 17, 18, 24, 27, 28, 30, 32, 52, 81, 82
Semevsky, V. I., 62–68, 105
Sergeyevich, V., 35, 42, 43, 53, 105
Shalyapin, F. I., 48
Shakhmatov, A. A., 79–81, 105
Shakhmatov, M. V., 99
Shashkov, S. S., 77
Shchapov, A. P., 68–71, 77, 103, 105
Shcheglov, I. V., 77
Shcherbatov, M. M., 11–13, 14, 15, 27 passim
Shilder, 67
Sibiryakov, I., 77
Slavophile school, 14
Slavophiles, 32, 37, 42, 49, 50, 51, 72, 103, 104; and Westerners, 32–36
Slavophilism, 36, 47, 60
Slovtsov, P. A., 75, 76
Society of Marxist Historians, 56
Solovyev, S. M., 36–41, 42, 44–45, 46, 48, 51, 52, 55, 59, 72, 83, 101
Spassky, G. I., 75
Spencer, 59
Speransky, 78
Stalin, 89, 94
Stalinism, 91
Storch, 10
Stroyev, P. M., 20, 21
Struve, P. B., 99
Svatikov, S. G., 99
Syechenov, 64

Tagantsev, N., 44
Tarlé, Professor E., 85, 96, 97

Tatishchev, V. N., 2–5, 14, 16, 41, 81
Thierry, 29
Tikhmenev, P., 79
Trotsky, 95
Trotskyism, 91, 95
Turgenev, A. I., 26
Turgenev, I. P., 22

Uspensky, 63
Ustryalov, 68

Vaghin, V. I., 78
Valuyev, 34
Vanag, 95
Varangians, 10, 30, 35

Vasilevsky, 63
Vernadsky, G. V., 99, 102, 103, 104
Vico, Giovanni, 37
Vinogradov, 84
Vladimirsky-Budanov, 43

Westerners ("skeptics"), 28, 32, 40, 50, 51, 59, 100, 103
Westernism, 36, 47

Yadrintsev, N. M., 76–77, 78
Yanson, 62
Yudin, G., 77

Zabelin, 35

Augsburg College
George Sverdrup Library
Minneapolis, Minnesota 55404